LATIN AMERICAN POLITICS IN PERSPECTIVE

MARTIN NEEDLER
University of New Mexico

Revised Printing

VAN NOSTRAND REINHOLD COMPANY
NEW YORK CINCINNATI
TORONTO LONDON MELBOURNE

Van Nostrand Reinhold Company Regional Offices:
Cincinnati, New York, Chicago, Millbrae, Dallas

Van Nostrand Reinhold Company Foreign Offices:
London, Toronto, Melbourne

Manufactured in the United States of America

Published by Van Nostrand Reinhold Company
450 West 33rd Street, New York, N. Y. 10001

Published simultaneously in Canada by
D. Van Nostrand Company (Canada), Ltd.

15 14 13 12 11 10 9 8 7 6 5 4

TO

LORE

AND

STEPHEN

Grateful acknowledgment is made to Professor William C Andrews for his advice and encouragement; to my wife and so to whom the book is dedicated, for their patience and forbearanc to Miss Susan Stoudinger for her services as typist; and to th students and lay audiences in New Hampshire and Michigan wh stimulated and corrected the ideas that became the content of thi book.

M. C. N.

Ann Arbor
May, 1963

Contents

Introduction

WHY STUDY LATIN AMERICAN POLITICS?

IT SEEMS only fair to begin a book with a statement : the author's reasons for presuming on the reader's time. The riter on Latin America may find himself under varying degrees : constraint on this score, since public interest in the area waxes nd wanes markedly in response to the vicissitudes of international olitics, rising if today's crisis is a Latin American one, dropping hen the headlines concern a country in the Eastern Hemisphere. Vhy should the conscientious North American[1] feel he ought to now what goes on in the countries to the south?

One often hears the argument: these countries are after all our osest neighbors and so should have first call on our attention; and uch is written and spoken that starts out from the premise that e United States and the countries of Latin America are indeed eighbors, living next door to each other in a single hemisphere. Iow this argument may have some force if one is referring to Mexo, Central America, or the Caribbean. It is rather weak, though, as pplied to the countries of South America—the major cities of Brazil : Argentina are closer to those of West Africa, for example, than ey are to the cities of the United States: Buenos Aires is 5800 miles om New York, and only 3000 from Dakar, Senegal; Natal, in the razilian Northeast, is only 1800 miles from Dakar. In fact, New ork is closer to Moscow by air than it is to Buenos Aires.

[1] "North American" rather than "American" is normal usage, and is prerred, in the Latin countries of the hemisphere.

The argument that Latin America is important to the Unite States for economic reasons makes more sense. There is an impre sive list of materials, from abaca to zinc and from balsa wood lead, which come to this country from the republics to the sout And yet, there are sources for almost all of these products elsewhe in the world—and for all of the important ones—whereas for ma of them substitutes could be developed if necessary. (On the oth hand, the United States is certainly important to Latin America— takes over half of the exports of two-thirds of the republics, and su plies over half of the imports of a similar number.)

To United States foreign policy, Latin America does prese special claims. Years of loyal support in international bodies; in t realm of political forms, the flattery of imitation; intimate acquai ance with the benefits and drawbacks of heavy North Americ investment: these have created psychological links and historic tachments which imply some sort of special consideration.

Quite apart from its significance to the student of foreign polic however, Latin America is, or should be, of great interest to t student of comparative politics. The existence of 20 republics of co parable culture, most of them independent for a century and a ha suggests a wealth of political experience that can be mined to yie valuable insights and fruitful hypotheses.

THE MANNER OF APPROACH

In dealing with a group of countries that have some characte istics in common, one can choose either to stress their similarities their differences. Each method has its strengths and weaknesses: lay emphasis on the differences and consider each country individ ally involves repetition and may lose the insights that come wi truly comparative work; to focus on similarities, on the other han means to minimize or overlook significant variations among cou tries and may create in the student the illusion of familiarity whe there is only superficial acquaintance.

This book adopts the comparative approach, organizing the m terial by topics and laying stress on those features possessed in co mon by the countries of the area. It is the author's belief, howev hat for a sound knowledge of Latin American politics a thorough-going acquaintance with the politics of the individual countries is iecessary *in addition to* comparative study by topics[2]; in his own eaching he has found it possible to combine both methods with ncouraging results. To derive the maximum intellectual return on iis investment, the reader is strongly advised, in addition, to become is familiar as possible with the geography of the area.

In following a topical and comparative outline, and in trying to lo justice to the complexities of the subject within the brief compass of this book, the intention has been neither to be overwhelmed by nasses of data nor to overwhelm the reader with them, but instead o use specific data as examples of principles, that is, to tie together pecific material by what may perhaps pass, in the primitive state of he art, for theoretical structure. It is hoped that any sacrifice of letail that this may have entailed will be compensated for by the eader's being able to make some sense, when he finishes the book, of Latin American politics.

The focus of the book, by way of contrast to others on the same ind similar topics, is on the regularities of informal political life ather than on the provisions of formal institutions of government or on the general cultural factors that relate to politics. It is the author's own feeling that this difference of emphasis helps to redress the imbalance that now exists in the literature on comparative Latin American topics.

WHAT DO THE LATIN AMERICAN COUNTRIES HAVE IN COMMON?

The differences among the countries that are considered here are substantial enough that it will scarcely be possible to make a generalization without immediately noting a list of exceptions to it. If one wished to stress the variations among the countries of the area, and not their similarities, he would have powerful arguments on his side. "Latin America," after all, includes Uruguay, whose inhabitants are Spanish-speaking, of European stock, and whose government is a

[2] For a country-by-country treatment, see Martin C. Needler, ed., *Political Systems of Latin America,* Van Nostrand, Princeton, 1964.

stable and peaceful democracy; it includes Paraguay, a country o mixed European-Indian inhabitants who speak Spanish and Guaran and who have always lived under dictatorship; it also includes Hait where the people are of African descent, speak a dialect of Frenc and have lived for the most part, one has to say, in a state of anarchy and it includes Brazil, whose language is Portuguese, and whos forms of government have been as various as the biological inhe itance of its people. If Brazilians, Haitians, Uruguayans, and Para guayans are all Latin Americans, how can one generalize? What d the various republics have in common?

Politically speaking, they share the following characteristics, amon others. In the first place, they have all had the experience of bein colonies of a European Power, being ruled from abroad throug the agency of a class of resident foreigners who monopolized th positions of local authority. With the exception of those in Brazi and Haiti, the institutions of government were similar in all th colonies. On the whole, the republics share the geographic charac teristic that communications are made difficult by natural bar riers—mountains, deserts, jungle—so that the population of the coun tryside perforce participates little in the political life of the capita (On this point one would have to except Uruguay and Argentin outright, while modifying its application in some other cases.) Thei economies are similar in that all are dependent to a greater or lesse extent on the production of primary products—that is, agricultura or mineral products—mainly for export, and therefore are sensitiv to fluctuations in international commodity prices.

In addition, the republics of Latin America share a common po litical consciousness, an awareness of what is happening to eac other, which can make developments in one country of direct influ ence elsewhere. If a dictator in one country falls, the dictator o another sleeps less comfortably; the words of a great democrati leader in one republic will evoke a response in the hearts of th citizens of a neighboring state.

Finally, the states of the area are similar in finding themselves, o the whole, at a comparable stage of political development. The ıave all passed through the stage of defining basic constitutional tructure that follows immediately on independence; they have all ıad to reach some kind of *modus vivendi* between Church and tate; they have all had to cope with the problems confronted in assing through the early stages of labor organization. Today they re all involved—or are shortly to be involved—with the problems f trying to reconcile the processes of democracy not only with olitical stability but at the same time with the requirements of apid economic growth.

It is the author's own belief that this last point is the most important of all, and that the history—in some cases, the contemporary istory—of countries on other continents supports him in the view hat the politics of the Latin American republics are simply the olitics of states at a certain series of stages in their political evoluion. The reader will find, accordingly, that the concept of "political levelopment" recurs throughout the discussion that follows, while rom time to time parallels are pointed out with the experience of tates outside the area.

I Political Culture

THE term "political culture" has been used to refe[r] to the totality of the factors, not themselves political, which deter-mine the environment in which political processes operate: the tra-ditions, attitudes, or normal patterns of behavior and thought tha[t] condition political action. The leading features of Latin America[n] political culture considered in this chapter will be: the heritage o[f] colonial rule, the state of those social factors that affect a country' stage of political development, and the nature of the issues that hav[e] formed the matter of political controversy in the period since inde-pendence from the colonial Power.

A. THE COLONIAL HERITAGE

It would be an error of the first magnitude, in any attempt to un-derstand the politics of the Latin American republics, to overlook the powerful influences exerted on them by three centuries of colo-nial rule. Let us consider in turn the political institutions and atti-tudes handed on from the colonial period, the political implications of the inherited patterns of social behavior, and, finally, the role of the Church.

POLITICAL INSTITUTIONS

The political forms that the Spaniards brought to the Americas were those of a particular time and place. To appreciate this is at the same time to understand much about them. They were, after all, by and large the institutions that Spain herself had at the end of the fifteenth century; in other words, at a time of absolute monarchy, of national unification, and of the expulsion of the Moors from

Spanish soil. It is a nice symbolic fact that the year in which Columbus "discovered" America, 1492, was also the year in which the Moors (that is, the Muslims from North Africa and the Near East who had added the Iberian Peninsula to the empire established by the successors to Mohammed) were finally forced out of the peninsula after centuries of warfare.

The national unification of Spain took place along lines similar to those followed in the unification of the other European states of the period. This was the time of the transformation of a feudal Europe, with its sharply stratified society, its elaborate network of mutual rights and obligations, and its multitude of local rulers owing vague allegiances to King, Emperor, and Pope, into a Europe of states, sovereign and equal, each ruled by a more or less absolute monarch who worked out the terms under which the Catholic Church should be permitted to conduct its affairs within his realm, if at all.

The strategy of national unification necessarily required that the king break the power of the local lords and the traditional autonomy of their domains. In this struggle, the monarch found natural allies in the burghers of the towns; for trade would surely stand to benefit by the policy of national unification, with its concomitant abolition of the internal tariffs and arbitrary exactions of a fragmented feudal society, and its improvement of communications. In return for their aid in the common struggle, the king re-confirmed the cities' self-rule charters or granted new ones, undertook to respect the autonomy of the guilds, and perhaps granted the city representation in the councils that advised him. The nobility, for its part, would be centralized at the Court, the nobles being transformed from rivals for power into royal civil servants or soldiers, or ineffectual courtiers.

As has always happened, before and since, national unification carried with it its own ideological force, a concept of national purpose and a feeling of national vigor which, with the mission of unification accomplished, looks beyond the national borders for new tasks in which to affirm its destiny. The ideology of the new Spain, matured in the long struggle to free the national soil of the infidel, could only be a militant and missionary Catholic Christianity. With the Reconquest, then, Spain was ready to go on to conquer a new world for trade, for the royal house, for the faith. It only remained that the new world be discovered.

Amplifying the Reconquest into the Conquest, as the theater of military activity moved beyond the seas, it was natural that the institutions appropriate to the one be adapted to the other. The fusion of political and military authority forged out of the necessities of frontier government on the marches of Christian advance in the home country continued in the offices of captain-general, governor, *adelantado,* that were conferred on the men who won the New World for Spain. Together with the auxiliary task of spreading the faith, that combination was quite appropriate to the needs of conquering new lands for Spain in America.

Colonial ways have left a lasting imprint on government in Hispanic America. In the colonies political authority and military command were joined; today most of the Latin American republics have still to create a military service separated from politics. Governmental authority in the colonies, as in Spain, was highly centralized and absolute; so it is in the republics. Law was the command of a sovereign who owed responsibility only to God and his conscience; today most of the Latin American legislatures are subservient to executives that are only nominally co-equal.

As in the mother country, the town enjoyed a certain degree of self-rule, and the town council (*cabildo* or *ayuntamiento*) was the only public authority that—at least at some times and in some places—was outside the executive chain of command. Because of this, the councils necessarily figured prominently in the Independence movement and the early governments of the republics. Today, it is usually only in the cities that one finds sustained participation in political processes.

Under Spanish rule, at least until shortly before Independence, mercantilist practices prevailed, with all colonial trade oriented to the mother country and inter-colonial dealings forbidden. The separateness of the colonies thus encouraged, which reinforced the formidable natural barriers to communication, helps explain the separate existence of the republics of today, whose boundaries generally follow those of the colonial administrative divisions of 200 years ago. In addition, many of the characteristics peculiar to the populations of each of the republics can be shown to derive from variations among the regions of Spain from which the colonists of each state came.

The independent states also inherited the colonies' responsibilities to religion, many of them continuing the special status of the Church that had existed under Spain.

Not all of present-day Latin America was under Spanish rule, however. As an eventual result of the Treaty of Tordesillas, in which the Pope arbitrated rival Spanish and Portuguese claims, and of the energy and initiative of Portuguese colonizers, the vast domains of Brazil came under Portuguese rule. Of the quality of Portuguese colonial rule, one might say in general that it rested more lightly on the colony than did Spanish rule elsewhere in the hemisphere, although the institutions of government in the two empires were comparable. The Portuguese in America, like their descendants there today, were more easy-going, less insistent on religious orthodoxy, more tolerant of local initiative than the Spaniards.

In French-ruled Haiti, on the other hand, life on the plantations was on the whole very harsh for the African slaves imported to replace as laborers the aboriginal Indians who had rapidly died out as the direct or indirect result of the severity of colonial exactions. Of course its quality varied with the character of the individual slaveowners, but the French were typically harder masters than the Portuguese. The treatment of colored freedmen in Haiti, at first generous, deteriorated as they came to outdistance the *petits blancs,* the poorer whites, in wealth and accomplishments, resulting, by the end of the eighteenth century, in an onerous system of legal disabilities, discrimination, and segregation.

The colonial mold has surely left its impress on the substance of political life in the republics of present-day America. It would be incorrect, however, to treat the nature of the colonial heritage as in itself sufficient to account for the features of politics in the area today. Characteristics of the colonial pattern that were appropriate to the changing circumstances of the republics remained, were strengthened, and were exaggerated; those that no longer had a function disappeared, or survived only as isolated anachronisms; while totally new practices grew to supply new needs. The active factors in the process were the requirements of time and place, the impact of crucial events and personalities, and the logic of the situations that developed. But much of the colonial pattern retained its relevance in the years that followed Independence: and that portion exerted its influence over the new, so that today an appreciation of the colonial heritage remains a prerequisite to an understanding of contemporary political life.

SOCIAL BEHAVIOR

The society founded by the Spaniards was, of course, a class society. The Spaniards came to conquer and to rule, not to work with their hands. The medieval conception of the nobleman whose only proper tools were the sword and the word of command was very much alive among the new arrivals in the Americas. To be sure, there was no need for the newcomers to labor, for the Spaniards conquered large bodies of sedentary people who could be put to work.

Here lies one of the crucial differences between what happened in English- and in Spanish-speaking America. The invaders from England found a few nomadic Indians not permanently settled in any one area, who could readily be driven off. At the same time, the thrifty Puritans who emigrated to the New World were ready and eager to work the new-gained land themselves. The large populations of sedentary Indians to the South, by contrast, could hardly have been expelled; and in any case the Spanish conqueror was not at all interested in doing his own farming and mining. Quite naturally, therefore, the Spaniards related to the Indians, whose land they were taking, as an upper class in a highly organized class society.

Thus, the type of society that each set of invaders found in its half of the New World was adaptable to the type of society conforming to the predilections of each. The English Puritans, independent and hardworking at home, could remain so—could become more so—in America; the Spanish *hidalgo,* or his lower-class imitator, aspired at home to the dignified and genteel way of life he found himself able to live in the colonies.

There were regional variations from this general organization of colonial society, however. In the Caribbean tropics, on the islands, and in the lowlands of the surrounding coastal areas, the Indians proved intractable as plantation workers, dying, escaping into the back country, or refusing to be captured in the first place. Here Negro slaves were imported, as they were to Brazil from the vast Portuguese African domains, and today the African strain predominates in these areas. What Indians inhabited the areas of present-day Argentina and Uruguay, on the other hand, were nomadic, and could not be made to serve as the lower class of an agricultural society. There the Indians met the same fate as those in the United States, being driven out or exterminated, and the land was settled almost exclusively by Europeans, as largely occurred also in Costa Rica.

The combination of these social factors with those of climate and terrain led to the three basic types of rural economy which, in general, one still encounters in Latin America. In the Indian-less countries of Uruguay and Argentina, one finds economies based on livestock-raising, needing much land and few workers. The tropical areas, by contrast, the lowlands of Northern South America and the Caribbean, grow plantation crops—sugar, bananas, cotton—usually on large economic units worked by the descendants of the indigenous peoples and of African slaves. Elsewhere, Indians and *mestizos* (those of mixed European and Indian ancestry) are found as workers in the mines, and on the *haciendas* (landed estates), and sometimes their own small farms, growing corn and vegetables.

The Spanish blueblood's attitude toward work is still current in the Latin countries of America. The upper-class Latin American generally has a casual attitude toward the obligations of his job that comes as a surprise to the North American (as anyone who has tried to make an appointment to see a Latin American colleague can testify!) The strength of this attitude varies from place to place, however, and the inhabitants of some of the more industrial cities of the area pride themselves on being more businesslike than their compatriots in the national capitals.

Similarly, the attractive careers for the Latin American student are those involving cerebral activity only, and that of a less demanding type. The universities are full of students of philosophy, poets, and apprentice politicians. There are lawyers enough to go round, and the supply of would-be men of letters more than meets the demand. Agronomists, statisticians, and rural schoolteachers, on the other hand, are less in evidence. As industrialization progresses, however—and it is well under way in Argentina, Uruguay, Brazil, Colombia, Mexico, and elsewhere—these attitudes presumably will begin to give way.

The relatively greater importance of the family in Latin America than in Britain or the United States should be mentioned in any discussion of the traditional social patterns that survive to affect political behavior today. Family connections are of importance in Latin America (as in other areas of the world, of course) to a greater extent than in the United States, and that means not simply the "nuclear" family of immediate relatives, but the extended family of cousins three or four times removed. Feelings of special loyalty extend also to those related not by blood, but by virtue of being godparents to the other's children (*compadrazgo*). One's *compadres*, like one's relatives, are entitled to special consideration. With this set of attitudes, nepotism and family favoritism become regarded as an almost legitimate obligation rather than as an illegitimate betrayal of trust. An officeholder is likely to regard loyalty to a "public interest" as a nebulous and unreal obligation that must take lower priority than the natural loyalty one feels to flesh-and-blood relatives. This type of attitude is maintained and strengthened b 'arious functional imperatives that will be discussed below in the ection on the public administration.

HE POSITION OF THE CHURCH

The strength of the Church, and of Catholic Christianity itself, aries markedly from one republic to the other. Whereas Protestant-sm or Judaism nowhere in the area constitute serious rivals to Catholicism (although Protestant missions are active in several coun-ries, especially Brazil), a rival of a kind exists in Haiti, and to some xtent in Brazil, in the cults derived from the primitive religions of Africa, which survive among some Latin Americans of African lescent. In Haiti, Voudun retains a claim on the allegiance of prob-bly most of the dwellers in rural areas, while the Brazilian equiv-lent, "spiritualism," has a substantial following among the poorest 0 per cent in the cities, as well as in the country.

Some purists have pointed out that often the Christianity of the boriginal American is heavily dosed with practices owing their rigin to religions of the pre-Columbus period. Re-baptised Indian leities have often found a place in the local Christian hagiology; vhile local variations in the celebration of Christian holidays are :vocative of heathen practices.[1]

It remains true that loyalty to the Catholic faith is strongest in he more Indian states of America, and weaker in the more Euro-pean and African. The most secular state in the region, for example, s Uruguay, with its population almost 100 per cent of European lescent, where the public calendar does not even carry the religious iames of the national holidays—December 25th is "Family Day!" ndian-and-*mestizo* Ecuador, on the other hand, has been called 'the land of churches," and was once dedicated by Presidential lecree to the Sacred Heart of Jesus (as was Peru also). The Indians'

[1] The skeptic might remark, apropos of motes and beams, that observations of this type are made with unconscious irony by those whose own Christmas eatures the fir tree of the ancient Germanic religion, or whose celebration of Easter involves such primitive heathen fertility symbols as eggs and rabbits.

loyalty to the Church may derive in part from the Church's role in protecting them, or attempting to, from the worst exactions of the civil authorities in colonial times, or it may simply reflect the greater religiosity of a primitive people living close to nature and the soil.

The political position of the Church itself has undergone considerable change over the years. One might fairly say that during the colonial period the Church was an integral part of the political-military-religious Establishment, with a role to play in the maintenance of the colonial system. As a corporate body—that is, as it acted through its formal hierarchy—the Church was a partner of the royal administration. Itself a landowner, the largest in the colonies, its bishops connected by ties of blood to the ruling classes, the Church found itself consistently on the Conservative side of issues under Spain and in the Independence period.

The parish priests, however, lower down in the hierarchy, could identify themselves with the cause of the lower classes. The father of Mexican independence was a priest, Father Hidalgo. (Before being executed he was defrocked, however, as was his follower Father Morelos.) One had a similar case more recently in the fight of Father Ramón Talavera against the Stroessner dictatorship in Paraguay, without the (overt, at least) support of his superiors in the Church hierarchy.

The identification of the Church with the forces of social conservatism, in general, continues to this day, but has been mitigated by two complementary developments. In the first place, the Church, since the "social encyclicals" of Leo XIII, has taken a position on social questions compatible with attempts to ameliorate the conditions of life of the working classes. Since the end of World War I especially, Christian Democratic or Christian Social parties have been founded, in Western Europe and Latin America, which favor the secular claims of the Church (for example, to participate in the education of the young) but which are at the same time socially progressive. Until then, one implicitly assumed that a pro-clerical political position entailed a conservative view of social and economic questions. Parties of this type have already achieved a leading position in the politics of Chile and Venezuela. In the second place, the Church has discovered that the twentieth-century dictator, in his continuing attempt to achieve ever more totalitarian authority, must sooner or later come into conflict with any organized body that remains outside the range of his control, including the Church itself. This will happen, experience has shown, no matter how favorable to the Church the dictator's initial acts will seem, nor how much the Church tries to "render unto Caesar": the totalitarian claims of modern dictatorship must necessarily end by invading the sphere the Church holds to be its own. This happened toward the end of the Perón period in Argentina, as it did during the term of Rojas Pinilla in Colombia.

Although a formal separation of Church and State exists today in several of the republics—the most important of which are Brazil, Uruguay, and Chile—the more usual pattern is for some kind of official recognition of Catholicism as the dominant religion, together with mild grants of government favor in the form of subsidies for church schools and the like. This is in normal times the situation in Argentina, Peru, Colombia, and Costa Rica, for example. In a few Latin American states, the Church has been subject to jealous vigilance and occasional persecution; in Mexico and Ecuador, for example, where the extent of anti-clerical feeling is probably a reflection of the degree to which the Church has historically attempted to intervene in secular matters; and currently in the Caribbean dictatorships of Cuba and Haiti.

One of the complaints that anti-clerical governments in the area typically make is that Church education and other activities weaken patriotism because so many clerics are foreigners (generally Spaniards; Frenchmen and French Canadians in Haiti). On the other hand, the opinion of foreign observers—since Independence especially, but even before—has been so unanimous in its condemnation of the average levels of intelligence, morality, culture, and general worthiness of their office of native priests, that one is inclined to be cautious about the merits of any program of expulsion of foreign-born clerics, on this as well as on other grounds.

B. RACE, CLASS, AND POLITICAL DEVELOPMENT

THE CONCEPT OF POLITICAL DEVELOPMENT

The temptation is apparently irresistible for the foreign observer to make quantitative and qualitative comparisons among the Latin American states. This is not an idle temptation, for much can be learned by comparison that could not have been learned any other way; at the same time, systematic comparison provides a way of ordering and organizing a large body of data so that it becomes understandable and usable. Presumably because democracy and stability are the attributes most generally held to be desirable, comparisons with respect to them are the most frequent. One distinguished political scientist and observer of the Latin American scene has conducted periodic polls among his colleagues in recent years to discover their assessment of how democratic the states of the area were in comparison with each other.[2]

A difficulty of using "degree of democracy" as the dimension in which one makes comparisons, however, is that it is susceptible of sudden and drastic change. A *coup d'état* in Cuba or Colombia may send the country from the head of the list to somewhere near the bottom; a successful revolution may move it from the bottom to somewhere near the top, literally overnight. On the other hand, stability, as a comparative measure, has the fatal weakness that there are two very different types of stability (a fact that U. S. foreign policy has very infrequently shown itself able to appreciate), that of the peaceable constitutional democracy, where revolts rarely or never occur because everyone can feel generally satisfied with the political order, and confident that it will do him justice; or the stability of the iron-fisted dictatorship, which rules by terror and

[2] Professor Russell Fitzgibbon. His article describing the results of the latest survey appeared in the *American Political Science Review* for September, 1966.

deceit, and which, last as long as it may, is likely only to serve as prelude to eventual anarchy and bloody civil strife.

Clearly, what is wanted is a standard of comparison that will discriminate among differing degrees of democracy without being prone to sudden mutations; that is sensitive to the difference between genuine stability and counterfeit; and can perhaps take account of some other variables as well. Let us assume that such a dimension of comparability exists and call it "political development." One would then say that *one country is more developed than another if it could be expected to be, normally, more democratic and at the same time more stable,* even though at any given moment it may have departed from its normal position; just as sharp fluctuations of a variable on a graph may nevertheless take place around a clearly visible trend line. The components that enter into calculations of "degree of political development" will then be those underlying characteristics that correlate highly with democracy and constitutional stability but that change only slowly over time.

Let us examine the concept further. Democracy entails general participation in political processes. This certainly means awareness of the national political life, fluency in the national language, and presumably literacy, since the newspaper remains a major device for producing familiarity with the national political process. Newspaper circulation, then, provides one rough index of political development. So does the number enrolled in schools, since literacy and level of information are factors.

Another index that reflects the state of some of the same variables is degree of urbanization—the proportion of the population that lives in cities; for participation, actual or vicarious, in national political life is in Latin America much more an activity of city-dwellers than of people in the countryside. The more people that live in cities, the more that are likely to engage in industrial occupations; so an index of degree of industrialization will be suggestive of the degree of political, as well as that of economic, development.[3]

[3] The appropriate figures for some of the indices mentioned are given in Table I.

Vicarious participation in the common life of the national community is at the same time, of course, the matrix for the complex of feelings known as nationalism, and nationalism is in fact a typical feature of the period of transition from a traditional to a modern way of life.

Although political development is correlated with democracy, this is true only in a general way. That is, a politically developed society may still be transformed into a dictatorship—as the history of twentieth-century Western Europe clearly shows. But dictatorship in a developed society is characteristically different from its counterpart in a traditional society. Traditional dictatorship is content to rule over apathetic and indifferent subjects who merely demonstrate no overt signs of disobedience. Dictatorship in modern societies, on the other hand—those of Hitler, Mussolini, or Perón, for example—aspires, where it reasonably can, to be totalitarian. That is, it starts from the assumption that the citizens will participate in politics. Rather than attempting the impossible, and trying to turn back the clock and impose an indifference to politics, totalitarianism accepts the fact of popular participation, but forces it into channels of support for the regime. One is not forbidden to vote, but compelled to vote—for the single candidate; and lack of inclination to vote or to attend meetings or rallies of the appropriate pro-government organization is interpreted as a sign of opposition to the regime and punished as such.

Political development is normally cumulative and permanent, then, and so serves as a steadier measure of long-term progress than other yardsticks that are susceptible to wide short-term fluctuations.

The creation of a national political community may proceed by many avenues, and a variety of secular changes may show, on examination, development aspects. Land reform—the transfer of the ownership or control of land to those who work it—has all kinds of economic and political meanings, many of which we will deal with below in a different context. But land reform also contributes to political development by conferring responsibility on those who have never borne it before, impelling them, for reasons of economic necessity, to have dealings with the larger world, in whose affairs they must then interest themselves.

THE POLITICAL MEANING OF RACE

It can hardly escape observation that the most highly developed countries of Latin America politically are at the same time among the most European in the ancestry of their population—Uruguay and Costa Rica. The most Indian and African states, on the other hand, are more frequently found toward the lower end of anyone's scale of political development, with either Haiti or Bolivia at the bottom according to any index used—literacy, level of income, newspaper circulation, or any other. Now of course race in a biological sense has nothing to do with this. Today, one surely does not need to point out that no innate biological differences can be presumed to exist that account for social and political differences of this type. The point is rather that "race" in Latin America does denote a certain cultural history and, even today, a distinctive way of life.

The political life of the modern republic in Latin America is, after all, a European invention. Presidents, parliaments, and parties are importations to the New World. Political business is conducted in the European languages, in the cities which were and are the centers of European settlement. To say that over half the population of Guatemala is Indian is to say that a substantial part of the population cannot speak the national language, never reads a newspaper, cannot understand a Presidential speech, does not leave its native districts, and has hardly any contact with national political life. To vary the example: the people of Haiti, the first republic of the 20 present-day Latin American states to gain its independence, are of African descent; the biological fact has no political meaning by itself until one adds the historical gloss that the Haitian people gained sovereignty at virtually the same time as release from slavery; they were illiterate, untutored, and without civic skills or the means of developing them. This is the political meaning of "race" and statistics on race as they relate to progress in political development.

When the Spaniards came, they found three major Indian civilizations in the New World where large sedentary bodies of population lived at an advanced stage of cultural evolution, the Aztec, the Maya, and the Inca. The successor states of these indigenous empires are today the countries with the largest numbers of unassimilated Indian inhabitants—Mexico, Guatemala, Ecuador, Peru, and Bolivia, reading from north to south.

One assumes that, sooner or later, genuine social transformations—that is, revolutions in the real sense—will take place that will bring about the full participation of the indigenous inhabitants in the political life of their countries. The successful Independence movements were not of this character. They were civil conflicts among the Europeans, with the Spaniards born in the New World, the creoles, winning their freedom from Spaniards originating in the Iberian peninsula itself, the *peninsulares*. Even in Mexico, where the Independence movement had had roots in the Indian population, it was soon taken over by the creole upper classes.

Genuine social overturns having as consequence the admission of Indians to the national community are taking place in Mexico, beginning with the Revolution of 1910, and in Bolivia, dating from the Revolution of 1952. A revolutionary process in Guatemala that might have ended with similar results was cut short in 1954 with the overthrow of the Arbenz Guzmán government, and the *status quo ante* restored. Ecuador and Peru remain leading candidates for social revolution, accordingly, as Guatemala does for a renewal of hers.

The admission of Indians to the national political community does not mean necessarily that they occupy positions of political leadership *as Indians*. If the example of Mexico, the state furthest along in this process, is typical, it is the *mestizo,* the person of mixed ancestry, who dominates politics at the expense of both European and Indian. As the Indian is progressively assimilated into the national community, rather, he loses his character as Indian, and becomes simply another Mexican. For example, in the conservative Mexico City daily newspaper, *Excelsior,* news of the Indian predominates on the first page of the second section—in the news of

TABLE I *Some Social Characteristics of the Latin American States*

	Life Expectancy (years at birth)	Daily Newspaper Circulation (per thousand)	Gross National Product per capita ($ US)	Major "Racial" Groups (in order of relative size)
Uruguay	66.5	185	560.9	European
Argentina	65.0	155	799.0	European
Costa Rica	59.0	94	361.6	European
Cuba	59.0	88	516.0	European, mulatto
Panama	56.5	76	371.0	Mestizo, mulatto, European
Venezuela	55.0	78	644.5	Mestizo, mulatto
Chile	54.5	119	452.9	European, mestizo
Brazil	54.0	54	374.6	Mulatto, European, African, mestizo
Paraguay	54.0	37	193.2	Mestizo
Mexico	53.5	115	415.4	Mestizo, Indian, European
Nicaragua	52.5	66	288.4	Mestizo
Peru	51.5	47	268.5	Indian, mestizo, European
Colombia	50.5	56	373.4	Mestizo, European
El Salvador	50.0	49	267.5	Mestizo
Honduras	47.5	20	251.7	Mestizo
Dominican Republic	47.0	27	313.2	Mulatto, European
Ecuador	45.5	52	222.7	Indian, mestizo, European
Guatemala	43.0	31	257.7	Indian, mestizo, European

TABLE I *Continued*

	Life Expectancy (years at birth)	Daily Newspaper Circulation (per thousand)	Gross National Product per capita ($ US)	Major "Racial" Groups (in order of relative size)
Haiti	42.5	6	149.2	African, mulatto
Bolivia	40.5	26	122.3	Indian, mestizo

NOTE: Figures on newspaper circulation refer to period 1959-63; GNP figures refer to 1961.

Sources: 1) Life expectancy, *Statistical Supplement* to the UN Economic Commission for Latin America's *Economic Bulletin for Latin America,* October 1962, cited in Bruce Russett *et al., World Handbook of Social and Political Indicators,* Yale University Press, New Haven, 1963.
2) Newspaper Circulation, *UN Statistical Yearbook,* 1964.
3) Gross National Product, P. N. Rosenstein-Rodan, "International Aid for Underdeveloped Countries," *The Review of Economics and Statistics,* May 1961.
4) Race, author's estimates.

crimes of violence. News of the Mexican of Spanish descent is found in abundance on page one, section three—the society columns. Page one of section one—the news of national politics—tells of the doings of the *mestizo.*

C. ISSUES IN THE EVOLUTION OF LATIN AMERICAN POLITICS

At any one time there will be a political issue, or an interrelated set of issues, which structure national politics. As conditions change, as new problems arise, as old problems are resolved or become obsolete, the central issue of yesterday's politics is replaced by another that serves in its turn as the orientation point of political activity. The parties measure off their positions to the left and right of the central axis; if the old parties refuse to adapt, new parties arise with programs focussing on the new set of issues.

It may be, as Seymour Martin Lipset has argued, that one of the key determinants of the structure of a party system and of the style of political conflict will be whether a polity solves its problems as they arise, clearing the slate to proceed to the next major problem, or whether it allows the divisions occasioned by problems of former years to continue, perpetuating the hostilities and party divisions of precious decades and even centuries, and thereby marring the functioning of the political process. Much evidence tending to substantiate this thesis can be found in the history of the Latin American republics.

It is possible without doing major violence to the facts to generalize as follows about the succession of issues that the political systems of Hispanic America have faced.

THE INDEPENDENCE PERIOD

During the first half-century of Independence, the problems faced immediately were those that concerned the basic organization of the new states: constitutional questions of centralism *versus* federalism, the right of secession, the form of the government, and the powers of the Chief Executive and how he should be chosen. To be sure, questions of this type occasionally appear even today; but a century and a quarter ago they were the major issues to be faced. Then the party struggle was Centralist *versus* Federalist,[4] or, as the parties usually adopted the nomenclature then general, Conservative *versus* Liberal.[5] Often, to be sure, the struggle would be based on personal ambitions rather than on questions of principle, and even when questions of principle were primary, personal ambition would not be far behind (as of course it never is, in party politics). Party combat was at the time, on the whole, physical combat, for several rea-

[4] Outside the United States, a "federalist" is invariably what we would call states' righter.

[5] In Argentina the Conservatives were federalist. Elsewhere they favored strong central authority, as in the early United States.

sons. In the first place, Independence had been won by warfare, an the leaders of the new states were generals who naturally turne to force as the arbiter of disputes. In any case, no peaceful pro cedures for solving disputes existed—the disputes themselves wer precisely over the machinery of government that should be con structed; to accept a mode of settling disputes peacefully woul already be a settlement of the substance of the disputes themselve How could a secessionist accept the decision of a *national* tribunal Why should the believer in a strong executive, elected for a lif term, a sort of republican monarch, debate the merits of his case i a legislature he believed should never have been called?

Eventually, the basic issues at stake here were settled, usually b violence, more or less definitively. The general outlines of the con stitutional systems operating today were already visible 100 years ag National boundaries were at last settled in most places, althoug Cuba and Panama only became independent in 1902 and 1903, re spectively. Boundary disputes continue to exist, of course, but the are between established states whose existence itself would not b placed in jeopardy by the adverse settlement of the territorial issu in question.

During the initial period after Independence, however, issues c actual national existence were basic ones. The countries of Centr America constituted a single federation from 1823 to 1839. For pa of the same period, Colombia, Venezuela, and Ecuador constitute a federation under the name *Gran Colombia.* Argentina did n acknowledge the independence of Uruguay until 1851 and had in tially attempted to include Paraguay within her borders.

THE RADICAL PERIOD

The themes of Latin American politics in the second half-centu of Independence were of a different character. One might call t years 1860-1925—very roughly speaking—the "Radical period"; t issues that dominated politics were those that figured in the pla forms of the Radical parties founded at the time. In some countri such as Argentina or Chile, separate Radical parties were founde ı others, such as Uruguay or Colombia, the Radicals simply formed ne tendency among partisans of Liberalism.

Radicalism meant, in the first place, laicism—that is, opposition) any role for religion in the life of the state.[6] This anti-clericalism, s it is usually called, had always been one of the basic principles of ineteenth-century Liberalism, but was stressed more heavily by the adicals. Radicalism also meant political reform, perhaps complete onstitutional overhaul, but certainly reform in election procedures. might also mean the beginnings of labor and social legislation—ut only the beginnings, for the Radicals were not workingmen by nd large, but professional people: lawyers, schoolteachers, and journalists typically, though with a sprinkling of "enlightened" businessmen and skilled workers.

Let us consider the points in the Radical program one by one. nti-clericalism is a policy not generally understood by North mericans, accustomed to the separation of the two kingdoms and nfamiliar with religious intervention in politics. Anti-clericalism pposes the Church on various grounds, the importance of each ırying somewhat in accordance with local circumstances. The hurch's role in educating the young is always abhorrent to the adical intellectual who regards it as imposing a bondage on the ind of the young contrary to liberal principles. At the same time, may object to the Church's possession of extensive lands—in some untries they constituted up to a third, or even more, of the arable ea—as an impediment to economic progress; whereas the Church's emption from taxes he believes throws a heavier burden on the ore productive segments of the population. That is, economic and eological motives may mingle, as they will do, to form a middle-ass anti-clericalism of businessmen, teachers, and journalists; those ncerned with economic as well as intellectual freedom. Accordgly, it was the usual pattern (though not in Argentina) for Radil or Radical-Liberal governments at least to separate Church and

[6] In Peru, the Radical movement stressed instead the elimination of military ervention from politics, and the party became known as the *Partido vilista.* Anti-clericalism did not become a major issue in Peru.

State, for example, as Alessandri did in Chile, or even to confisca Church property, as Juárez did in Mexico. The Radicals also o jected to religious monopolization of the rites that signal the maj events of the life-cycle, and they supported civil marriage ar burial, the civil registration of births, and the permission of divor

Progressive leaders of the Radical period were also very mu concerned with electoral and constitutional reform. Batlle y Ordóñ in Uruguay and Alessandri in Chile were particularly strong a vocates of constitutional change, and each was responsible for l country's getting a new constitution, Uruguay's being adopted 1919 and Chile's in 1925.

The Radicals were interested in electoral reform not only f ideological reasons, to be sure, but also because, since they enjoy greater popular support than did the conservative and landowni classes, they could expect electoral success proportionate to the re resentative quality of the elections. The Conservatives, on the oth hand, suspected the same thing, and regularly kept themselves power by manipulation of the election machinery and restriction the suffrage. The Argentine Radical Civic Union had made hon elections one of the central points in its program from its foundi in 1890, for example, while the slogan of Mexican liberalism the ouster of Porfirio Díaz after 30 years of rule in 1910 was t same as it had been at his accession: "effective suffrage—no election."

The Radical movement did not run its full course in all the cou tries of Latin America; in most of them, for a substantial part the "Radical period," political development was interrupted by d tatorship and free political activity was interdicted. Where polit was free, however, the central issues were those that Radicalism h made its own.

Of course, this was the Radical period in all the independ states of the West, and there is a strong family resemblance amo all the Radical and Radical-Liberal movements that flourished this time, and indeed among their typical leaders: the popular he ex-journalist, -professor, or -businessman, with a dynamic persona d a touch of demagoguery and dictatorialness, liberal and idealic but careful to stop well short of socialism. Irigoyen in Argena, Alessandri in Chile, were surely cut from the same cloth as emenceau, Lloyd George, and Woodrow Wilson. Batlle y Ordóñez viated from the general pattern somewhat in lacking the dictaial personality and in being prepared to go further to the Left his social policies.

E RECONSTRUCTION PERIOD

In 1922, Mussolini's Fascist movement took over the government Italy. In 1924, a young Peruvian intellectual named Haya de la orre founded APRA, the American Popular Revolutionary Allice, a movement of the democratic Left. The key problem of the cceeding years was to be the alleviation of the economic misery, arpened by the worldwide Great Depression, which gave fascism opportunity, and the democratic Left its leading task. The proams written in these years were blueprints for the uplifting of down-trodden; most of the new parties founded were either cist or social liberal of the APRA type. Indeed it seemed at times if some of them tried to be both, like the National Revolutionary ovement (MNR) of Bolivia.

Many of the old-style dictators of the area took on fascist trappings d fashioned some home-made fascist ideology to try to become entified with what the misguided of the time thought was "the ve of the future"; Getúlio Vargas in Brazil, for example. But this s no more than a case of keeping up with the fashions, and when styles changed the outmoded clothes were put away. In some untries—Mexico, Chile, Brazil, Ecuador, Bolivia—new movements nuinely fascist, in doctrine, uniforms, and style of political action, re founded; but these never became serious contenders for power. ly in Argentina, with Peronism, was there a movement authenally owing anything to fascism that had a lasting impact.

Parties similar in orientation to the APRA, on the other hand, ich were founded during this period, have come to play the minant role in Mexico, Venezuela, and Costa Rica, as well as in

Bolivia and in Peru itself. In addition, countries without a domina party of the APRA type have had *aprista*-like Presidents who ha inaugurated "New Deal" programs.

Of course, this was the period of the world struggle against f cism, culminating in World War II, which had an indirect but po erful influence on Latin America itself. Economically, the war ye were years of economic boom in Latin America, as the United Sta turned increasingly to countries of the area to supply raw materi for the war effort, many former sources of which were then unc Axis control. At the same time, prices for the peacetime exp products of the area were abnormally high, due to their relati scarcity under wartime conditions. Furthermore, the unavailabil of many manufactured products formerly procured from the Unit States and Britain gave an impetus to the development of local dustry, especially in the larger countries of the area, which had sizeable domestic market.

The central issues of the period 1925-50 were thus those stemmi from economic reconstruction, on the one hand—over social sec rity, labor organization, and government regulation of the econo —and, on the other hand, those over international diplomatic a ideological alignment.

THE CURRENT PHASE

Since about 1950 the themes of Latin American politics have be different enough from those of the years immediately precedi that one can profitably speak of a new period in the politics of area. That is, while the processes of politics have not necessar changed, the central issues are significantly different from th of the immediate past to the extent that the period merits separ treatment.

The focal issues of the last decade, and surely of the two or th decades to come, are those centering on the problems of econor development and of the cold war. The two issues have many poi of intersection with each other, but are, of course, analytically qu separate.

n a general way, one can say that there has always been a con- n for economic development, and the period of 20 years or so ore the end of the nineteenth century, especially, saw a variety government actions motivated by this concern. Today, however, nomic development policy is clearly the central issue above all ers. This phenomenon is not confined to Latin America, but is te general in today's world; it comes about for several reasons.

n the first place, the tremendous rise in the rate of population wth must be held a contributory factor. Given the steady in- ase in population, merely to maintain the current *per capita* level life needs a substantial expansion of employment opportunities l of national production. While the increase in the rate of pop- tion growth is taking place today generally all over the globe, it especially marked in Latin America where, for example, the hrate in Costa Rica is one of the highest national birthrates in world, according to current figures, and almost twice that of the ited States.

atin America, too, has shared in what has come to be known as e revolution of rising expectations"—that is, the new and grow- conviction among the less-favored peoples that it is not inevi- le that one live at a bare subsistence level, eking out a precarious l miserable life amid squalor and disease. To some extent, mod- communications techniques have contributed to this phenome- by acquainting the peoples of the southern half of the globe h the manner of living in the developed societies. The extensive bility of Europeans and North Americans has had a similar ct. In some cases, there was also the influence of returning vet- ns who had themselves witnessed the wonders of the modern rld in the course of their travels, or had at least acquired a rest- ness and an impatience with the old ways.[7]

oncomitant with the revolution of rising expectations, and itself

Mexico, Brazil, and Colombia have sent expeditionary forces to fight along- those of the United States in one or another of the wars of the twentieth ury. Bolivia and Paraguay fought the bloody Chaco War in the 1930s, le several other states have fought over border questions.

providing a stimulant to it, is the fact that in the present int national environment, the chances that foreign aid will be availa to assist a development program are very good indeed. Two relat factors are of importance here: the Cold War and the existence the United Nations organization.

The Cold War means several things in this connection. It mea that one or both of the superpowers may be ready to assist in development program as a way of attempting to insure against h tile acts on the part of a small state. It means that the general sta mate between the superpowers enables the small state to pursu line of policy independent of big-Power domination, each ma Power being reluctant to use extreme measures of coercion for f that they may lead to general war, or at least to a local installm of such a war; or that they may drive the small state and sympathizers into an alliance with the main adversary. It may a be possible for a small state to ally itself with one of the ma Powers and extract substantial amounts of aid by raising the spec that without aid revolution may come, with the consequent form tion of a hostile government; or by urging the advantages of to create a "showcase" of the beneficial effects of the social syst that the small state allegedly shares with its big-Power patron.

The existence of the United Nations General Assembly, in wh each small state has a voice and a vote, and thus the partial abil to inflict "propaganda defeats," gives the small state's plea for in its development program a certain weight it might not ha otherwise. At the same time, the specialized organs of the Uni Nations can themselves provide modest technical assistance that v be less subject to the charge that it constitutes foreign intervent than assistance which bears the character of aid from one state another.

The institution of an economic development program entails n mally the adoption of several types of government policy; cen planning and state investment, with concomitant controls on e nomic activity of various types, together with revision of the structure; the encouragement of foreign investment, private or p

:, or both; a policy of stabilization of the value of the currency, kely otherwise to become inflated as the development program enerates new purchasing power without producing new consumers' oods in its early stages; and perhaps changes in the organization the agricultural sector.

The problems of economic development policy will be surveyed detail in a subsequent section. But clearly, an economic develop-ent program will provide plenty of issues for political controversy. he lines of division that such issues impose on the politically active opulation may well be related to the lines that form over Cold 'ar questions. With the creation, with the later developments in e Cuban Revolution, of a government in the Americas that leans ast in the Cold War, Cold War issues have taken on relevance r inter-American relations. That is, one's attitude toward the esent government of Cuba has become itself a pseudo-Cold War sue, and makes of immediate concern other issues of the Cold 'ar proper, which would surely otherwise not have intruded them-lves into the domestic politics of the Latin American republics ith such force.

Over these questions in current controversy, as over the key issues other periods, new parties have formed, mostly small pro-Castro opular socialist" groups[8] made up of college students and other oung people. Usually negligible in appeal to the voters, these are significance principally when they establish a para-military arm, hose "guerrilla" tactics of bombings and kidnapings can cause real arassment of the democratic process, especially in providing ounds for the military overthrow of a government thought to be oft on Communism." Terrorist and guerrilla activities by the far eft have been common recently in Guatemala, Peru, Venezuela, e Dominican Republic, and Colombia, with less important

[8] The designation "National Liberation Movement" or "Front of National beration" is also common; the Costa Rican Party of National Liberation, e should note, however, antedates this use of the term, and is *aprista* and t pro-Castro; the National Liberation Movement of Guatemala is a con-vative party.

groups functioning intermittently elsewhere. A generalized fear o Communism stimulated by the upsurge of activity on the Left ha been one of the factors responsible for the assumption of power b Right-wing military officers in recent *coups* in Argentina, Brazi Ecuador, and the Dominican Republic.

This concludes our brief survey of the development of the ke issues of Latin American politics, and of the parties that grew ou of the conflicts described. While many of the issues discusse achieved some kind of definitive settlement, others did not, and con tinue to exist today in modified or attenuated form, like the Churc State controversy in some countries. The parties that developed ou of specific positions on the issues of the day in some cases disap peared together with the issues that gave them birth; in some case they continue to exist, trying to keep alive issues of little relevan to new national problems; in yet other cases they have found ne issues on which to appeal for popular support; while sometimes o course the party continues in existence without real issues, as simple alliance of assorted politicians for electoral purposes. Wha type of fate awaited the different parties depended in part on th political, and especially the electoral, environment in which the operated. This, together with the position of the parties today, wi be considered in a subsequent section.

I Political Processes

A. PERSPECTIVE

XPLAINING LATIN AMERICAN POLITICS

How does one go about *explaining* why Latin American politics ıkes the forms it does? There are no problems in *describing* the ıajor features of politics in the area: the central role of the military, ıe prevalence of violence, the ascendancy of dominant personalities ather than the sway of impersonally functioning institutions, the ɪidespread graft and nepotism—these are the commonplaces of comıentary. There are commonplaces of interpretation, too, but their ower of explanation no longer compels, if it ever did. Latin Amer:an authors themselves have traditionally been free with "racial" xplanations that cite alleged deficiencies in the Indian races, or in eoples of mixed blood; these are largely out of fashion now, even ı Latin America. Economic and cultural explanations, on the other and, are still popular: the gulf separating social classes, poverty, literacy, lead to a politics of desperation and violence, one reads; lternatively, the colonial past, or the heritage of the Iberian peninıla itself, can be shown to have set the patterns of authoritarian ule that persist today.

Explanations along these lines, however, while plausible enough ı long as one considers only the American republics themselves, ıse their force when one tries to apply them on a wider scale. Poverty and illiteracy have after all been the rule in human societies, in ıe stable and orderly ones, too; while on the other hand a politics f violence, a "Latin American" type of politics, is becoming visible ı countries that have never known Spanish or Portuguese rule.

Consider for a moment recent events in the former Belgian Congo independence from the colonial Power is followed by a struggl between federalists and centralists; a charismatic *caudillo,* Patric Lumumba, is captured by his rivals and, predictably, the *ley fug* is applied in the classic Latin American manner—he is shot "whil trying to escape."

The reasons for the existence of the major features of Lati American political dynamics become clearer if one takes a rathe different perspective, one that places at the forefront of the inquir the fact that the stability of a system of political institutions rests o an acceptance of those institutions as legitimate.

In a stable polity, that is, the maintenance of order does not res routinely on the application of force. Force is kept in reserve, o course, to put down the occasional violations of the peace; bu normally political life moves in well-marked channels, in accordanc with pre-adjusted patterns of behavior. This is, surely, true by defini tion since this is what we have in mind in speaking of a stabl political system. Now in the short run, in an immediate sense observance of the rules of the game, willingness to stay within th marked channels, is a matter of habit. One does what is customary one follows precedent. In the long run, however, when out-of-the ordinary circumstances arise, when methods of handling new situa tions must be devised—that is, when new institutional patterns o behavior are to be created—then existent patterns are reproduced, o new patterns are created, because they conform to accepted ideas o legitimacy. These ideas will be peculiar to the time, and perhaps t the place; nevertheless, they will be accepted as natural and righ For example: a group of North Americans organized in a club o society are faced with the necessity of making some collective deci sion. They take a vote, and the majority preference becomes th group decision. Perfectly natural to us; yet strange and repugnan to Samoans, who, we are told, allot decision-making power only t heads of extended families; or to traditionalist Indonesians, wh prefer to talk things out until a consensus is reached; or even to ou own ancestors of four centuries ago.

'o carry the reasoning a step further: one obeys a person in ıority because he has come by his office in the proper manner; manner which is established by precedent, of course, but which is "right" in being based on accepted principles of legitimacy.[1] m this point of view, the features of political life traditionally acteristic of Latin America derive from the existence of what ht be called a "legitimacy vacuum." The Latin American states passing through a period of transition between one set of principles of legitimacy and another; during the period of transition some ures have survived from the old way, some have developed as cursors of the new, but for the most part legitimacy does not ch to existent institutions. In the absence of stable patterns of timate political behavior, no alternatives exist to the dominance ersonality, the absence of public spirit, and the rule of force.

TIMACY IN THE COLONIES AND TODAY

he central feature of the colonial legitimacy system in Latin erica was that political power, like social status, depended on acknowledgement of the rights of birth. This was clearly true ıe very top rank of the political order: the monarch came into title by inheritance. The legitimacy of the tenure of office of rior authorities, in turn, rested on royal appointment, and so the le structure of authority derived legitimacy from this inherited . But social status conferred by birth constituted the normal equisite for the holding of high office in any case; moreover, leading offices in the Spanish colonies were reserved for Spans born in the peninsula itself, rather than in the New World, ughout virtually the whole of the colonial period. The scope of s political functions, then, was defined by the rank into which was born.

Vhether one obeys or not will probably also depend on whether the in:ion is a lawful one, that is, on whether the official is acting in the way supposed, on whether he is staying within the bounds of our expectations his behavior. For present purposes, however, I wish to stress the idea of imacy especially as it applies to the right to hold an office, rather than to ehavior imputed to the office.

The nature of the role ascribed to the holder of public office flected this situation. The duties of upper officials were unspeciali and did not require tedious training or the acquisition of skills becoming to a gentleman. At the top of the local colonial hierar administrative roles were actually not even differentiated into arate political, military, and religious categories, the colonial ernor being responsible for saving souls and leading military c paigns as much as for collecting taxes and keeping the road repair. The minimal technical skills that were necessary were r larly provided by the clergy, who formed an integral part of governing system.

Authority in this system, then, came from the top down, deri from the rights of birth, and ultimately from God's grace. T sure, there were occasional ambiguities over the details of the r governing the precedence of different degrees of relationshi inheriting a throne, and there were, accordingly, succession cr Nevertheless, normally the inheritability of the position of supr authority, like the criteria of status based on birth that applie eligibility for lesser positions, made possible stability and contin in the political order.

Today, no one is "born to rule" in any place that is touche the modern spirit. In modern political systems, supreme auth can be derived legitimately only from popular choice. Legitin comes now not from "above" but from "below."

A whole series of lesser principles flows from this revolutio basic political values. Popular sovereignty presupposes and reinfo juridical equality and equality of social opportunity. Given equ of opportunity, the criterion of public personnel policy beco merit, not social status; while in a public service based on m technical specialization becomes possible (as it cannot be in a ser based on class), high standards of technical proficiency can be pected, and government can take on increasingly complex functi

If popular sovereignty thus makes the welfare state possible, it makes it probable—following the ancient Aristotelian maxim discovered by Harrington and again by Hamilton, that the dist n of property tends to mirror the distribution of power. That is, democracy is likely to redistribute property in the direction of uality (through a system of progressive taxation that supports cial services benefiting especially the poorer citizens, etc.).

One is thus likely to find the institutions of the modern polity cepted as legitimate not only because of the habitual acceptance mmanded by any stably operating political order, but also because vernments functioning within it—for electoral purposes, if for no ier—clearly attempt to govern in the interest of as wide a segment the population as possible; because of the general conformity of icial administrative actions to rational technical criteria; and because the popular will is obviously the highest authority in the state.

E "LEGITIMACY VACUUM"

With the fairly clear exception of Uruguay, none of the Latin nerican republics has emerged altogether into the modern period its political and social institutions. Some occupy a position not far m the pole of the colonial polity; others are clearly in steady gress toward the modern pole; and all combine some features of l and new, together with key characteristics of the process of nsition itself.

What has happened, in effect, is that the Wars of Independence cceeded in sweeping away the colonial system, in eliminating any ssibility of relying on the idea that legitimate authority comes m above, from the royal succession sanctioned by the grace of d, without replacing it by a system of practice based on the belief it legitimate authority comes from below, from the popular will. ntrast the American and French Revolutions, which had ended al authority to replace it with new conceptions of political right, nceptions that impelled a reordering of social institutions on the sis of the principle of equality. After abortive attempts in Mexico d Haiti, and a successful attempt in Brazil, at establishing indigeus dynasties, the newly independent republics became, regardless what their constitutions said, turbulent oligarchies, in which the ssession of power lacked that overwhelming legitimation that comes from its being derived from a great principle of right. Th locus of power at a given moment, accordingly, was regarded arbitrary and could be contested by whoever was able.

However, the constitution itself was nominally based upon th notion of popular sovereignty and embellished with mottoes take from the French and American Revolutions. But the social realit and operative social beliefs, were so strongly at variance with th doctrines expressed in the constitution, that the document necessari failed to provide an actual working guide for the political syster To this day, of course—to the surprise of North Americans—th Latin American constitution tends rather to be regarded as a stat ment of ideals, a set of aspirations, rather than a sober directive which political reality must conform.

Politics existed then and, for the most part, exist today in "legitimacy vacuum." In the absence of any compelling legitimatio of the right to hold office of the present incumbents, in many stat their term lasts as long as they can maintain themselves by force arms. In the absence of a set of operative ideals that inform t behavior patterns of everyday political life, cynicism predominat public office is used to promote private advantage, and nepotism a theft become cardinal principles of public administration. If the chi criterion of public personnel selection under the Crown was birt and in a democracy is merit, then in a legitimacy vacuum it is pe sonal loyalty. Because one's hold on power is so insecure, to rema in power becomes the all-important objective. One dare not ta chances, in such a situation, by relying on strangers; positions trust must necessarily be given to fellow-partisans and, where po sible, to relatives.

Where institutions carry no conviction, and where the bonds party are too often only those of self-interest, the single availab alternative focus of loyalty and faith is the individual leader: a personalism is of one piece with the lack of public spirit and t absence of a doctrine of legitimacy. Militarism, too, is an unavoidab concomitant. Where authority is not respected, force must be sorted to. Where force is used, the army necessarily has the l word. In this type of situation, the army is in politics whether it wants to be or not.

Looked at in this light, those distinctive features of Latin American politics that have been explained racially or culturally or economically can be seen rather to be attributes of a certain stage of political evolution, a time of transition, the period of a legitimacy vacuum. Accordingly, they can be found elsewhere, wherever polities must pass from a set of institutions based on one principle to another set resting on a different premise. One can find a "Latin American politics" in Europe in the age of the transition from the hierarchy of reciprocal obligation of the late Middle Ages to the monarchical sovereignty of the early modern period; or in Rome during the transition from republic to empire.

If this thesis has a meaning for the present time, it is that Latin American politics, in the present era, cannot become stable and peaceful, unless it is re-structured on the basis of the only contemporarily available conception of legitimacy—which is, today even more than a century and a half ago, popular sovereignty and juridical and social equality. When this is accepted as the basis of institutions and policy, a breakthrough into a new world of legitimacy is achieved. This was, at bottom, the nature of the change wrought by Batlle in Uruguay and begun by Carranza and Obregón in Mexico; in both countries, political stability came as a consequence of the development of a policy of social and economic progress for all sectors of the population within a democratic framework.

Often, in superficial analyses, the requirements of stability and those of democracy and social equality are opposed to each other. But, today, the stability achieved at the expense of democratic ideals can only be an optical illusion; it lives by force and will die by force. The basis for a stability that abides can today only be a foundation of democratic legitimacy, achieved by the institution of a regime which, in the process of policy-making and in the substance of policy itself, is responsive to the popular will. We shall return to this theme in the concluding section of this book.

B. THE PRESS AND PUBLIC OPINION

THE PRESS

Before discussing the character and political role of the Latin American newspaper, one should make clear that the term "the press" embraces a broad range of periodicals of widely varying quality, views, and political impact. The difficulty inherent in arriving at any fair over-all picture may be in part responsible for the dearth of any literature on the political role of the press in Latin America, despite its palpable importance.

One indication of the key role the newspapers play in shaping public opinion, if any were needed, can be found in the political importance of the newspaper publisher himself in Latin America. Examples come to mind such as Laureano Gómez, who has dominated Conservative politics in Colombia for 30 years; Pedro Beltrán, recently Prime Minister of Peru; or Harmodo Arias, whose control of a large portion of the Panamanian press helps to make him one of the three or four most important men in the country.

Although the range in quality of the newspapers of Latin America is great, one would probably be justified in saying that the over-all average, in terms of journalistic standards of objectivity of reporting and breadth of coverage, is low. Partisan bias and sensationalist handling of the news might be expected in the mass-circulation tabloids; it certainly occurs at that level in the United States, and in England too, despite the superb quality of the leading English newspapers. But one finds less-than-objective handling of news stories even in the respectable press—even *El Tiempo* of Bogotá, for example, which enjoys an international reputation, is not immune; while the deliberate distortion of the news one finds in *El Comercio* of Lima, the leading Peruvian newspaper, reaches astonishing proportions.

This feature of the Latin American press, the conscious or unconscious distortion of the news, is presumably due to the more emotional and more extreme character of partisanship in Latin American politics. The ultimate in the partisan affiliation of the press is probably reached in Uruguay, where Montevideo is served by 14 newspapers, each linked to a different political faction.

There is on the whole a conservative bias to the Latin American press, as there is to the press in North America, because of publishers' financial and psychological ties to the business community. A politically conservative, as well as sensationalist and pro-United States, tone is added by the general dependence on dispatches from the wire services of UPI, although many papers take the rather more balanced and accurate service offered by Agence France Presse.

The extent of everyday government regulation of the press seems excessive to the North American. The network of official regulations, many dating from colonial days, have as their ostensible aim the avoidance of immorality, defamation of character, and sedition. Clearly, such regulations are susceptible of abuse by governments desiring to limit the freedom of the press to be critical.

But there are many other ways in which government influence can be brought to bear on the press, and opposition journals made to feel the consequences of incurring official disfavor. Some of the devices that have actually been used in the Latin American states include the following, taken from the recent history of Argentina, Honduras, and El Salvador. The press may be required to print all government news releases, without comment, thereby being forced to surrender the bulk of its columns to official propaganda. Licenses to publish, or to practice the profession of a journalist, may be required, and may be withheld from unsuitable applicants. The government may monopolize the supply of newsprint, setting quotas a paper is to receive in terms of how compliant it is with government wishes. If newsprint must come from abroad, a similar purpose can be achieved by controlling the foreign exchange available to papers with which to buy it. The favorable rates at which public services—cable, telephone, mail—are provided to the press may be withheld from certain periodicals on a variety of pretexts. Applicable tax or minimum wage rates may be adjusted upwards. And so on.

Although outright censorship is often employed, governments prefer to avoid this if possible because of the sensitivity to the issue of freedom of the press in Latin America. In addition, a Freedom of the Press committee of the Inter-American Press Association exists, which makes a practice of drawing attention throughout the hemisphere to denials of press freedom.

PUBLIC OPINION

From what has already been written on social structure, it is possible to surmise much of the structure of public opinion. That is, in most of Latin America normally effective national public opinion is limited to the urban areas, and indeed confined for most purposes to upper-status groups. In recent years the leadership of organized labor has entered the circle of those whose opinions can be brought to bear on the policy-making process without resort to violence. On some occasions, in important elections or in revolutions, public opinion among the more quiescent areas of society can be mobilized, but this is not the normal day-to-day situation.

The divisions of public opinion follow class lines, social class being a more definite, more pervasive, and more important thing in Latin America than in the United States. They also follow party lines, the leadership being given by the party spokesmen and press.

The major single influence on the formation of political opinion in each country, however, is that of the government leadership, whose doings and especially whose pronouncements take up a much larger proportion of newspaper columns than is customary in the United States.

The second major influence on the formation of public opinion in Latin America is the Catholic Church. The influence of the Church hierarchy extends beyond questions of the relations of Church and State and may on occasion be brought to bear on the whole range of national political problems. Historically, this influence was exercised on behalf of the forces of order and the *status quo*. Those in authority are placed there by God; the troubles we experience in this world try us and prepare us for the next; to rebel against constituted

:hority because it does not alleviate, or worsens, adverse conditions hus sinful; and so on.

Clerical influence is especially strong among the rural people, for om the priest is likely to be the most educated man with whom y come into contact, and at the same time someone whose funcns are a vital part of their daily lives. Clerical influence in the es, especially among women, should not be underestimated, how-:r.

The Church's identification with the forces of order was never olute, though, and there have been signs in recent years of an :nowledgement of the grievances of peasants and workers as itimate, and an acceptance of organization and political action as ans for their remedy. Catholic trade unions have been a feature :he labor world for nearly half a century now, although they have l a substantial membership only since World War II.

n addition, as was mentioned above, the Church has in recent rs been forced through experience to realize that eventually supt of a modern dictator or even passive failure to oppose him olves it in self-abasement and acquiescence in plainly immoral ctices; but one may be pardoned for reserving judgment on the :stion of how well the lesson has been learned. The Church broke h Perón, and later, with Trujillo, only after it had been directly ıcked following mild protests at being pushed beyond all tolerable its. The record of the Church in Colombia with respect to the e of Rojas Pinilla is better; in the case of the present Paraguayan tatorship, the most favorable judgment is that the Church hierhy's position has been ambiguous, although individual priests 'e made clear their opposition to the regime.

There is currently in progress a resurgence of clerical activity in itics, even in Mexico, where the Church had recently been purng a policy of caution and non-involvement. The occasion for this :he promotion of a strong anti-Communist offensive, prompted the favorable attitude toward Communism and the Soviet bloc wn by Fidel Castro, and designed to counteract incursions of *:lismo* in other states of the Americas.

Fidelismo itself forms one of the currents of popular opinion day, based largely on long-standing anti-Americanism on the L To a large extent, being pro-Fidel Castro today is simply the curr way of being anti-American, in that Fidel has defied the Yank and has thus far "gotten away" with it. It is more, and less, th that, however; it is also one of the current forms that youth idealism takes, and is most marked among the youth, especially the universities.

The anti-Americanism that exists is perhaps only what could expected of countries that find themselves in juxtaposition to colossus whose every act affects them vitally, and might ruin the while he is hardly aware of their existence. Porfirio Díaz has be quoted as having said "Poor Mexico! So far from God, and so cl to the United States." That this overwhelming proximity is the k factor here is strongly suggested by the fact that precisely the sa type of anti-Americanism can be encountered widely in Canada.[2]

Anti-Americanism on cultural grounds, with the theme that No Americans are cultural barbarians, is found especially among intellectuals, of course. Marxism—in its cruder forms—is met w too, also principally among the intellectuals, although some sim fied versions have filtered down to elements of the politically c scious working classes. From a Marxist or pseudo-Marxist viewpo the United States is objectionable as the leading capitalist state, course; and Marxist views—especially Lenin's theory of imperiali as a stage of capitalism—can be made to dovetail fairly neatly w traditional Latin American anti-Yankeeism, though it would still a mistake, and quite misleading, to confound the two.

Public opinion is also structured by region. Regionalism is stro within most Latin American countries; natural barriers to co munication, especially the great mountain ranges, segment nati into self-conscious regions. Very often regional differences

[2] A Canadian statesman has remarked that Canada ought to begin a tec cal assistance program to the African and Asian countries to teach them a Americanism, seeing that Canada is the oldest and most experienced pra tioner of the art.

entuated by ethnic differences going back before Columbus; be-een the Quechua- and Aymará-speaking areas of Bolivia, for ex-ple, hostile feelings are traditional.

A common situation is for inter-regional tension to be dominated an overriding rivalry between the two leading cities, or between y and hinterland.[3] Inter-city rivalry is strong in Brazil (between de Janeiro and São Paulo), in Colombia (between Bogotá, Cali, l Medellín), in Ecuador (between Quito and Guayaquil), and is ipient in Mexico (between Mexico City and Monterrey). The ond city has grown because it is favorably located for industrial commercial development, as a rule, and is more business-minded, l indeed business-like, than the capital. Thus, the bustling *ulista,* or the hardworking *Antioqueño* (from Medellín), com-ins of the laziness and inefficiency of the people in the capital, rt and enmeshed in red tape, and not pulling their weight in the nmon effort.[4] There is business activity in the capital, of course—fact Mexico recently embarked on a program to try to get industry rted outside the Federal District, where it is concentrated—but arger proportion of it is in commercial, banking, insurance, and er service types of activity, and not manufacturing, than in the ond city.

C. GROUPS IN THE POLITICAL PROCESS

E POLITICAL ROLE OF ORGANIZED GROUPS

For the student of politics, the important thing about social groups the political role they play. Accordingly, it will help to bear in nd several basic distinctions. In the first place, one should dis-guish between "groups" that are simply aggregates of people con-iently described by the same set of terms, and "groups" that are

The latter rivalry should be familiar to North Americans, being typical of itics at the state level, although the former, rivalry between the two leading es, characterizes the politics of Missouri and California.

In Brazil this situation will presumably be modified in the future by the ent move of the federal capital to Brasilia.

actually organized, with a leadership structure and specific comm interests that give rise to common political aims. Thus one can d cuss Latin American children of school age, or Bolivian Preside of the nineteenth century, as "categoric groups," as aggregates people with common characteristics who can be considered togeth they are not "purposive groups," with leadership, organization, a specific functions to perform. It is with purposive groups that we a at present concerned.

The type of political activity in which groups engage will clea depend on the stage of development at which the country's politi life has arrived. As the country progresses further from the turm that followed its establishment as an independent state, as it develc political institutions capable of resolving disputes by peaceful mea —assuming that it ever does—the methods of political activity b come those appropriate to a stable and peaceful society. This chan in appropriate political techniques means a change in the types groups that are important in the state's political life. Obviously, force is the only technique usable in settling disputes, for examp the army will be of crucial importance. The political importance the army, accordingly, diminishes as a state develops politically.

However, force in politics need not consist only of fighting pitch battles. The general strike, for example, is a use of force that m be effective, and organized labor can wield political power even an era dominated by violent methods. Other groups, too, may be a strategic position to make effective use of the strike, as the secti on political violence below endeavors to make clear.

In the succeeding stages of political evolution, then, ability to u techniques other than those of violence becomes more important determining the role a group will play in politics. As voting streng becomes substituted for fighting capabilities in measuring a grou bargaining power, numbers assume a new significance. The imp tance of sheer numbers, however, will be modified by other factc This is obviously the case where suffrage is limited, say to t literate, as is currently the case in Brazil, Chile, Colombia, Pe and Ecuador.

The importance of sheer numbers is also modified by the relative presence or absence of the appropriate skills among the group's leadership. For example: the National Confederation of Popular Organizations, one of the three "sectors" of the government political party in Mexico, does well for itself out of proportion to its membership in intra-party bargaining over party nominations to office, in part because its leaders are especially skilled in the arts appropriate to successful private negotiations. One recalls the aphorism that the United States has never lost a war and never won a peace conference.

A final variable that will help determine a group's relative political importance is the extent to which the group's claims are consistent with the felt imperatives of national interest. That is, if it is the settled policy of the state to pursue a program of economic development requiring the expansion of domestic industry, local businessmen are in a strong position to press their political claims. If an increase in the number of people speaking foreign languages were clearly in the national interest, say, the teachers of foreign languages would find themselves in a strong tactical position.

BUSINESS GROUPS

There are several features of the activity of business interests as political groups in Latin America that deserve special mention. Typically, there exists in each of the republics a general association of business leaders in manufacturing and commerce that will concern itself with public issues that affect business as a whole. General labor legislation, for example, would be one such issue.

For many purposes, however, associations of firms engaged in specific types of activity, and individual businessmen, are more likely to be involved in the formulation and administration of any given governmental policy than the business community as a whole. This takes place because most government action that affects the country's economy will have varying impacts on different types of business. A country's tariff, for example, the formulation of which is one of the key areas of public policy as far as business interests are concerned, typically applies different rates to different items of trade.

Each manufacturing industry lobbies for protection from foreign competition for its own product, and while the interests of different industries may well coincide on tariff questions, they are often in conflict. Similarly, different industries may oppose each other on tax questions, saying in effect "Tax him, not me."

Moreover, business is also interested in government contracts, and here, of course, activity is necessarily on an individual firm basis, with firms competing with each other for government favor. Subsidies and special economic legislation of all kinds likewise come in this general category.

If one were to group businessmen in terms of their political orientation, however, the following broad classification might have some merit. The first business group, which might be called "traditional," is composed of owners and managerial staffs of enterprises not engaged in manufacturing, but in the public utilities field, in railroads and shipping, banking, insurance, mining, and the representation of foreign interests. These are the traditional non-agricultural economic activities in Latin America; they are also those involving connections with foreign, that is, European and North American, business interests. Here representatives of the old upper classes are to be found, and often outlooks on life similar to those prevailing among the large landowners.

A second sector of the business community, the "new" group, let us say, is composed of entrepreneurs in industries that developed to serve the domestic market, especially during World War II, when consumer goods were in scarce supply from the industrialized countries, whose economies were engaged in war production. A comparable development, of lesser magnitude, had occurred during the first World War, and even a little earlier. As always in the first stages of industrialization, industries began first to provide goods that are in need even where the population subsists at a low level: food, clothing, and housing. The first industries, accordingly, are invariably food processing, soft drink and beer manufacturing, cement, and textiles. Some activity during this initial stage in the production of other articles of prime necessity—matches, cigarettes, and soap, for example.

During World War II, and in the years since then, however, the process went further than this, especially in Mexico and Brazil, the countries with the largest domestic markets, where today a wide variety of goods are produced, for domestic consumption and export to neighboring states. Argentina and Uruguay have also experienced considerable industrial development, dating from earlier in the century.

Businessmen of the "new" group come to a lesser extent from the old upper classes, one major reason for this being that the new industries are often located near sources of raw materials or power, or central distribution points, away from the capital.

Where he depends principally on the domestic market for his sales, the businessman of this type favors tariff protection against foreign competition, and is more likely to support moves of "economic nationalism" in general.

The third group within the business community might be designated "petty" business, comprising the self-employed in trade and services who are not themselves significant employers of labor. The taxi drivers, owners of tiny grocery stores, shoemakers, and so on, of this group, make up a surprisingly large proportion of the economically active urban population. At its margins, this group blends into the ordinary labor force, and the political aims and methods of its members are closer to those of organized labor than to those of other business groups. That is, members of the group lack direct personal access to individuals in high authority on the one hand, but on the other hand are numerous enough to have an impact at the polls, and by means of rallies and strikes. At the same time, the low income level of the petty businessman makes him highly concerned, like the laborer, with the general level of prices and of government benefits.

Quite commonly, one must point out, relations between individual firms and public officials in Latin America are based on bribery and betrayal of the public trust. In the dictatorships, the existence of this situation is well known, of course. Of the recent dictators, Perón in Argentina, Batista in Cuba, Trujillo in the Dominican Republic, and Pérez Jiménez in Venezuela, amassed fortunes reckoned in the hundreds of millions of dollars; Anastasio Somoza, in Nicaragua, became a millionaire probably on a lesser scale.

Graft through illicit government-business connections is not unknown in the democratic countries either; Brazil and Mexico, and Panama among the smaller countries, have a particularly impressive reputation on this score, although this is hardly a point on which comparative annual statistics can be published.

A great deal more "business graft" becomes available when a country embarks on a program of economic development. Fortunes can be made quite simply as an incident of a government program of encouraging the development of industry. Attempts have been made to justify "North American" graft of this type, which at least is associated with the productive use of government funds, as opposed to classic "Latin" graft which simply entails the plundering of tax revenues, with no economic development involved.

As an illustration of how "constructive" graft works, the recent notable case of a leading Mexican figure may be cited. This political leader, who once missed nomination for the Presidency by the merest accident, was given, together with a group of associates, a sizeable government loan to start a paper-making concern. The group was also given exclusive rights to cut timber in a national forest. Moreover, a prohibitive tariff was placed on certain foreign paper products, despite the fact that they were in short supply in Mexico. Government help on this extensive a scale is almost as good as a license to print money. From one point of view, this is corruption; from another, it is economic development and the industrialization process. After all, initial industrial development in Japan, and in the United States too, was heavily government-subsidized (and often still is). Thus the administration of President Alemán in Mexico (1946-52), himself now a very rich man, was on the one hand a period of colossal industrial growth and public building in e country, and, on the other, the era in which graft reached new ders of magnitude.

In general, then, business's political activity is more likely to be nducted by individuals, single firms, and single industries than on unified basis. In terms of the techniques business groups can emoy, clearly *by itself* the business community commands neither ilitary or para-military force, nor numbers of votes. Accordingly, e techniques business usually uses are those involving personal fluence, campaign contributions, and even bribery. If a reforming vernment, or merely one that is erratic and incompetent, threatens isiness interests severely, there are always suggestible members of e military establishment who can be contacted.

GANIZED LABOR

The age of the national labor movement varies, in general, with e country's over-all level of political advance. Labor unions as we iow them today go back to the nineteenth century in Chile and ruguay, whereas the union movements in Haiti and Honduras ive developed only since the end of World War II. The types of economic activity in which workers are engaged determines how feaile it is to organize them (this can be seen also in the United ates, for example, with respect to migrant farm workers), with ricultural workers being especially difficult to organize—because ey are not so concentrated into one spot; because the rural areas e out of the mainstream of national life; because agriculture is 's productive than industry and presents fewer possibilities of ›rkers' gaining through organization; and because of the political wer of the landowner class, which has often secured legislation aking union organization more difficult among rural workers, or tlawing it entirely. In about a third of the republics, there are still organizations of agricultural workers.

A substantial increase in the number of workers enlisted in union nks has been noticeable since World War II, following in part on e acceleration in the rate of industrialization during the war riod.

Transportation and public services exist, of course, even in the pr industrial era, although there may be legal prohibition of the unio ization of government employees and such services are often gover ment-provided. Nevertheless, railroad workers were generally o of the first groups to be organized in the Latin American countri sometimes preceded by the printers' trades. Restrictions on t organization of government employees are widespread, and ev where unionization is allowed, the right of public workers to stri is typically limited.

Organized labor has always been "in politics" in Latin Ameri since the early years, following the European pattern rather th adopting the traditional North American "business unionism" pri ciple of confining activities to securing economic benefits with minimum of involvement in party politics. European influenc were in fact strong in the Latin American labor movement in early years. Societies of handworkers existed as early as the midc of the nineteenth century with mutual aid and insurance purpos providing protection against sickness and burial expenses, and se ing as fraternal and self-help organizations. Workers' groups becar politically-minded under the influence of Spanish and Italian i migrants late in the century, taking on the utopian, anarchist, a syndicalist coloration of the early unions in France, Spain, and Ita that is, the dominant political doctrines did not envisage politi action within the society and polity as then constituted, but only apocalyptic act, sometime in the future—the general strike—to bri about the collapse of capitalist society and its replacement by so other type of society, conceived of in rather vague terms, whi would operate without compulsion and human exploitation.

Around the turn of the century, specifically socialist ideas beg to become progressively stronger in the labor movement, bei joined by a separate Communist tendency after the Bolshevik Re lution. The more militant Communist element, while always in minority, did become very potent during the 1930s, when Co munists occupied key positions in unions in many of the La American countries, as they did elsewhere too at the time. T ength has since receded, although not disappeared, as a result of 'eral factors: attrition in Communist ranks themselves as the basic quirement of loyalty to the Soviet Union took Communist parties ng a twisting and often unpopular line of policy; government licies on the one hand restricting the Party's activities or outlaw- g it altogether, and on the other hand pursuing a liberal line that dercut Communism's appeal; and a vigorous counterattack by mocratic socialist and left-liberal forces within the unions them- ves, with some aid from the North American union movement d the regional free trade union federation (ORIT). Separate ristian unions have also been formed in recent years, acquiring litical significance in Chile, and promising to become of increasing portance elsewhere, for example, in Argentina and Central nerica.

There are currently interesting but isolated cases of new labor lerations established with at least the intention of sticking to ead-and-butter economic activities and staying out of politics, in lombia and very recently in Mexico. One may perhaps be par- ned for viewing the prospects for a non-political labor movement Latin America with a jaundiced eye, however, since the growth the labor movement has in the past been very clearly related to vernment favor or disfavor. Thus, the most highly unionized publics—those with the highest proportion of manual workers tually belonging to unions—have been Cuba and Argentina. This te of affairs is clearly due to the official support of the union ovement in the 1930s and 1940s in Cuba under Batista, Grau San artín, and Prío Socarras, and in the 1940s and 1950s in Argentina der Perón.

The attitude of the government is crucial not only because it ablishes the ground rules that apply to the organization of unions ompare the differences between the effects of the Wagner, Taft- artley, and Landrum-Griffin Acts in the United States), but be- use it takes a hand in day-to-day union activity and collective rgaining. Typically, official approval is necessary for a strike; if e strike is declared illegal, strikers may be fired without reinstatement rights, and if the strike threatens to damage the nation economy seriously, the government may even suppress it by viole means. On the other hand, the government board charged wi labor conciliation may find that the demands of the workers a justified, and the President or the legislature may embody them decrees or legislation. The settling of a labor dispute by Presidenti decree is a common occurrence.

Obviously, under these circumstances, it pays heavy dividends be on good terms with the incumbent administration, which, for i part, will require in return loyalty from the union federation. Som times the government will take direct action to ensure such loyalt or at least to interdict anti-government policies, on the part of t unions. Argentine unions, for example, were "intervened" freely l Perón, in the days when he was establishing his control over t labor movement, and later by President Aramburu in trying purge the union leadership of Peronist elements. "Intervention" co sists of suspending the union's officials from their functions, whic are taken over by a government-appointed interventor.

The history of Mexican political life provides ample illustratic of official control of the union movement's being established l means of the favoring of one federation and one set of leaders ov another. During President Calles' term (1924-28), for example, t CROM, under Luis Morones, who became a sort of Mexican Jimn Hoffa, was given government protection and favor and waxed gre and arrogant. Morones was frozen out of his privileged positio however, by Emilio Portes Gil, Provisional President during 192 and subsequently under President Cárdenas official favor was a corded Vicente Lombardo Toledano, an intellectual who headed t rival CTM. Lombardo was too radical for Cárdenas's successors i office, though (the federation he now heads is affiliated with t Communist international labor movement), and he was forced o of the position of favored labor leader, yielding it to the prese general secretary of the CTM, Fidel Velásquez.

Labor organization in Latin America is covered, like many oth areas of activity, with an extensive system of public regulation, ofte f the most minute details of union affairs. Like other such detailed odes of regulation, however, it is typically only partially enforced, nd then politically, that is, government supporters are favored, pponents not. Working conditions, maximum hours of work, minimum rates of pay, retirement, sickness and disability benefits, and rievance procedures are covered by the labor codes; these codes are nforced often against large-scale foreign enterprises, rarely against omestic business, and hardly ever against rural landowners. The oreign enterprise, that is, is easy to regulate; highly visible, affluent nough to meet the terms specified by law, without popular domesic support, and with a rational accounting system that simplifies nforcement of the regulations.

As was noted above, governments in power favor labor not only ut of principle, but also in the expectation of benefiting from future abor support. Thus, the relationship between the two may entail ot only the protection and direct encouragement of unionization, ut also the subsequent organization of unionized workers in a proovernment political party. The early Revolutionary governments f Mexico had fostered the growth of a labor movement, and ubsequently the major labor federation affiliated directly with the overnment party, now the Party of Revolutionary Institutions, vhen President Calles founded it in 1928. Juan D. Perón, similarly, nade the fostering of new unions one of the primary policies of the arly days of his regime, and then used the unions as the basis for he *Peronista* Party. Likewise, Getúlio Vargas, the Brazilian dictator, ounded the *Partido Trabalhista Brasileiro,* after he had left the 'residency, out of elements supporting him because of his pro-labor olicies. During Fulgencio Batista's earlier period of dominance of Cuban politics (to 1944), he too built a political party, with the articipation of unions whose growth he had promoted. All of the 'residents cited came to power originally by violent means and ecured labor support only by virtue of the policies they pursued *fter* taking office.

Labor unions are in a strategic political position for various reaons, and increasingly governments in search of popular support have turned to organized labor. In the first place, labor can generally command a substantial bloc of votes in the balloting. In any case, the organized character of the labor movement, and the number of people whose mobilization for election-time and other political tasks it makes possible, is itself significant in view of the general lack of continuing party organization in Latin America. More important still is the power of the strike weapon, which can be used for purposes ranging from the backing up of a demand for a wage increase to the overthrow of a government. Accordingly, the position of the labor movement has become one of the central features in the politics of almost all of the Latin American countries. In the case of Bolivia for example, the tin miners constituted the key political force in the country for much of the period 1952-1964.

AGRICULTURE

In more than half of the countries of the area—all except Haiti Costa Rica, Cuba, Mexico, Bolivia, and Venezuela—the chief agricultural interest is that of the large landowner, the owner of the huge *fazenda, finca, estancia,* or *hacienda,* as it is variously known The landowner is a potent figure in national politics. The labor law are not written to cover the people who work for him, or if they are, they are not enforced. The tax burden rests but lightly on his shoulders.

In his country's politics the aim of the large landowner, as a class is to be left alone—that is, for the rural *status quo* not to be disturbed. In his view, the role of government with respect to agriculture should be supportive, not restrictive—to provide subsidies, tariffs, and loans whose repayment is not stringently insisted upon.

In the coastal lowlands of the tropical areas around the Caribbean one finds plantation crops—sugar, bananas, cacao, cotton—very often grown by North American concerns. Historically, these concerns too, had a powerful voice in politics and operated outside the law The government-manipulating exploits of the banana-growing buccaneer, Samuel Zemurray, in Central America, have long been re arded as typical of the operations of United States fruit companies. 'oday, although United Fruit and its subsidiaries and affiliates still oom large in the economies and politics of the Caribbean, governients that want to have learned how to domesticate the fruit companies. In banana-growing Ecuador and Panama, at least, the govrnment keeps United Fruit in its place, enforcing the labor laws, or example, against it even if against no one else. However, laws n Guatemala and Honduras are less restrictive toward United Fruit, nd governments there are more likely to consult with the company han to fight it. North American interests in agriculture have been xpropriated in Cuba, on the other hand, and largely so in Mexico. n Panama, United Fruit's subsidiary has even threatened to stop perations in the country if it is saddled with further financial bligations to the government or to its own workers. One cannot ssume that this threat is an idle one, moreover. United Fruit has ound it better economics to limit the bulk of its operations in Ecuador to shipping and marketing the stems, rather than growing hem, and is in the process of adopting this policy elsewhere.

Where the *hacienda* system is in full effect, agricultural laborers—he forgotten men of the nation—have no voice in politics. If thoroughgoing land reform should come, however, as it doubtless will o many countries in the area, the ex-tenants, -sharecroppers, or aborers receiving land under the program will gain a political voice long with the title to their parcel.[5] In Mexico the organized beneficiaries of the land reform constitute one of the sectors of the government political party, and any government must make a special ffort to be *agrarista* in its policies. In Bolivia, the *campesinos* (the easants), most of whom have seized land without waiting for the ormalities involved in receiving a title, are much more loosely rganized but still constitute one of the key elements in national olitics. These new landowners are interested in credit, irrigation

[5] The economics and politics of land reform programs will be dealt with at reater length in a subsequent chapter, in relation to its role in an economic evelopment policy.

projects, rural schools and perhaps extension programs, and pric supports. They also champion the right to receive land of thos peasants who have not yet benefited from the land reform.

In Haiti ownership of the land has always been widely distribute since shortly after Independence, and the problem of reform of th land tenure system has not arisen. The small landowner is als typical of much of Costa Rica, Panama, and some areas of Colombi although the precise figures are in dispute.

In Uruguay, until very recently, an unusual situation existe Agriculture—in this case principally livestock production—instea of being subsidized, directly and indirectly, as in most of the oth states in the area, was itself forced to subsidize Uruguayan industr Uruguay, under the Colorado party, had long followed the polic of favoring industrial development, but since the country's man facturing proved a high-cost enterprise, domestic raw materials an power not being available, it could only develop with heavy gover ment aid of various types. The ultimate source of this financing industry was government profits from the state's monopoly on agr cultural and pastoral exports. Uruguayan farmers would of cours sooner have received all the benefits from the export of their produc themselves, and rural dissatisfaction with Colorado economic po cies was one of the key factors in the defeat of the party in 195 after half a century in power. The Blanco regime has yet to demo strate that it can manage Uruguay's economy better—or even as we —as the Colorados, however.

The structure of a country's land tenure system depends in pa on the crops grown—tobacco and coffee, for example, can normal be grown just as profitably on a small farm as on a large on whereas sugar or cotton are more rationally cultivated on a plant tion basis—and this will in turn depend on the terrain, the soil, an the climate. For instance, the best coffee is grown in temperate hig land areas with porous volcanic soil, as in El Salvador or Colombi whereas the rolling grasslands of Uruguay are ideal for cattl grazing. Thus, specific local factors go to shape a country's syste of land tenure. One would nevertheless be justified in asserting th order for the Latin American countries to provide a healthy ;ricultural basis for economic growth, they must do away with *tifundia,* the extremely large estate only partially farmed by a iserable resident laboring force, using primitive, low-yield, tradi- ›n-bound methods.

The persistence of the *latifundia* helps maintain the whole tra- tional social structure, and creates problems for economic policy at will be considered in the final chapter. In political terms, it eans the presence of an extremely influential group opposed to rtually any kind of social and political change, whose power is ›solute on the local level in the rural districts of three-fifths of the publics, and on the national level in several of them.

UDENTS

Student groups are of key importance in Latin American politics. :udent politics are integrated with national politics; student body ections are fought among candidates identified with the national ›litical parties; leadership of a major student faction in the national ıiversity carries national political prominence; the holding of ected office in the student government is the first step in a political ıreer. At the same time, university issues become of national ıoment, and the chain of events that leads to the overthrow of a ›vernment may have had its origin in the appointment of an un- ›pular rector (the chief university administrator); while the Presi- ent of the Republic may find himself called on to decide how ıany applicants the Medical School should admit, or what the stu- ent fare on buses should be.

The Latin American university, with one or two rare exceptions, as little in common with the university in the United States, so ır as its organization and the status of its student body are con- erned. In North American universities, the administration, which separate from both faculty and student body and is normally re- ›onsible to an outside body of some kind, frequently prescribes etailed regulations governing the life of the student, often of a ighly paternalistic kind. Autonomous student life and student government have to do only with trivial matters and private soc activities.

The Latin American university is actually much more simil in many ways, to that of medieval Europe—that is, an association scholars regulating their own affairs. In fact, the oldest major insti tions of learning in the hemisphere—the Universities of San Mar in Lima, of Santo Domingo, and of Mexico City—date from t middle of the sixteenth century. However, contemporary stude participation in university government dates properly from the U versity Reform movement, which began in Argentina during t second decade of the twentieth century, and had as concomita aims the relaxation of academic regulations, the introduction extension programs, and the general democratization of the univ sity. Today, the Latin American university is not completely co trolled by the students, certainly, but they do have a share in actual policy-making and administration, and not only in triv affairs. For example, student participation occurs in the election the rectors of the several faculties (the colleges devoted to speci branches of learning). Student representatives commonly accou for between one-fifth and one-third of the membership of import university councils and committees.

Usually the government has a role in university administratio often designating the rector or at least representatives on univers boards. This means that the government is involved in univers politics, just as students are in national politics.

In effect, the student community in a national university, especia in the faculties of law, philosophy, and the social sciences (wher separate faculty for the latter exists), is the group that constitut with its alumni, the nation's political elite. The prominence of substantial number of the present political leaders of the La American republics began at the university. The current generati of leaders of the democratic parties in Venezuela, for exampl Betancourt, Leoni, Villalba—is heavily drawn from a famous gro of student leaders known as "the generation of '28." Fidel Castro R first came into public view as the candidate for the Vice-Presider the student body in the Faculty of Law at the University of avana, and his associates in his first act of rebellion against the atista dictatorship, the assault on the Moncada Barracks, were rmer fellow-students.

Some political movements have been organized among the stu-ents by their professors, sometimes initially as aids in a campaign r the office of rector. The present President of Bolivia, Víctor Paz stenssoro, organized his *Movimiento Nacional Revolucionario* as Professor of Economics in La Paz. Former President Grau San lartín of Cuba also organized his initial political following among s students at the university.

Because of the importance of student politics, one often finds ›perannuated nominal students prolonging their university course r past its normal term so that they can continue active in univer-ty politics, even deliberately failing their examinations if necessary maintain student status. Some individuals continue as students ore or less indefinitely, perhaps switching to a new field and start-ıg over after receiving a degree, waiting for the government to ıange to the control of their own party and for a political career open up.

Actually, appointment to a government job may well seem the ıly prospect for many students. Concentrating in the humanities, pecially literature and philosophy, and in law, students are not articularly being trained for the specialties in demand, while in ıy case there is typically general unemployment and underemploy-ıent in all sectors of the economy. An appointment to the diplo-ıatic service or to a post in the Ministry of Education may represent ıe only hope for lucrative employment to the undergraduate poet r philosopher; the lawyers are more versatile, but there are too ıany of them, also.

This involvement with national politics means frequent hiatuses ı the normal pursuit of one's studies. The student body may be out n strike in protest against a government, or a university, policy; ıe school may be closed by the government, as a precautionary ıeasure or in retaliation for a student strike or demonstration. Professors or students may be absent from the classroom under arre or leading a revolt, or presenting demands to the President. Studer from the United States have been known to give up in baffleme after trying unsuccessfully to pursue a course of study for a ter at a Latin American institution.

In recent years, there has been something of a trend to a mc North American type of university, in some respects, in the "unive sity city" movement. In half a dozen countries universities ha been relocated on campuses of their own away from their traditior home downtown in the national capital.[6]

The politics of the university student are in general more extrer than the politics of the adult world. Specifically, the student's poli cal orientation is more likely to be nationalist, Leftist, and Marxi This is so for various reasons. The idealism of youth, which o must surely commend without necessarily agreeing with the speci views to which it gives rise, means a position on the Left exce where strong religious feelings supervene; at the same time t intellectual apparatus of Marxism appeals strongly to the intellectu and its anti-U. S. implications make it still more attractive; wh the rebelliousness that naturally accompanies later youth is au mented by the gulf between the generations typical of the Hispar family.

At the same time, the class position and prospects of the stude have a great deal to do with his political outlook. The children well-to-do families frequently go abroad for their education, Europe or the United States. Fees in the national universities a

[6] The present writer is more than a little inclined to suspect that in cc structing "university cities" governments are not simply endeavoring to cre the most favorable environment for learning, but are also trying to save the selves a lot of headaches by de-politicizing the university, at least by getting away from the vicinity of the Presidential and Legislative Palaces and there insuring that a student demonstration will not automatically place the life the government in jeopardy. It may be relevant in this connection to note tl the trend to the "university city" has also entailed an emphasis on athlet which is totally new for Latin American universities, and may provide interest- and energy-absorbing alternative to participation in political demc strations.

ially nominal; students there are often poor, not only supporting mselves but also in many cases contributing something to their nilies—university attendance is normally a part-time proposition. other words, the student is often undergoing genuine hardship, rking too hard or too long at his outside job, and, as noted above, prospects for remunerative employment in his field at graduation slim. The resentment and frustration that grow from this situa-n contribute their share to a politics of emotional extremism.

Thus, one might almost generalize that the students are always inst the government, regardless of its complexion and policies. The more conservative faculties, as one would expect, are En-eering and Medicine. There the students are not so intellectual so socially conscious as those in the other faculties and can look ward to relatively easier access to prosperous careers.

The religious influence is stronger in provincial universities, which as a rule less politicized than those in the national capitals; but ditions vary so widely that it is hard to generalize on this point.

E URBAN POOR

n the last 20 years, the cities of Latin America have experienced enomenal growth. The doubling of urban populations during this iod has not been exceptional. The rate of growth of the cities has n so rapid that the supply of decent housing has been completely mped, and in many cases the provision of municipal facilities been strained past the breaking point. Guayaquil, in Ecuador, perhaps suffered most from the ills of urban population explo-n, but Rio and Caracas also show extreme symptoms, and no jor city is immune.

The new arrivals from the countryside improvise shacks out of atever materials are available, and settlements of such dwellings shroom around the outskirts of the city, unprovided with water, tricity, or sewage disposal facilities. Little employment is avail-e—the city population was rapidly expanding anyhow by the ural increase of its inhabitants—and the dweller in the *rancho* he *favela* lives in conditions of misery, hopelessness, and general social disorganization. There were already miserable unemplo and underemployed in the city, but now the order of magnitude the problem is changed.

The political activity of the slumdweller is at present minima he is apathetic and "alienated" from the political process—and to he is most logically considered as a social problem rather tha social force, as object, not as subject. This situation is unlikely last indefinitely, however.

D. THE ARMY AND POLITICAL VIOLENCE

THE VARYING ROLES OF THE ARMY

As everyone knows, the armies of Latin America are involved the politics of their countries. The precise nature of the involvem shows a good deal of significant variation, however, in kind as w as in degree, and the whole topic has been subject to much r understanding. We must then discuss the political role of the ar in Latin America in terms of the different types of "involvem in politics" that are possible for military organizations.

Minimal Involvement in Politics. Now, virtually any army is volved in politics at least as a pressure group acting in the inter of its constituents. That is, it is interested in the procurement of most modern weapons, in securing increases in pay and fringe b efits, in building officers' clubs, and so on. We are not unfami with this type of military lobbying in the United States, of cou nor with *sub rosa* contacts between military officers and legislat nor even with generals' making speeches on policy questions, spite the well-established doctrine of civilian control, and des repeated attempts of the civilian leadership to keep the milit confined to their professional functions.

In Uruguay this pressure group role is normally the extent military involvement in politics, and in Chile and Mexico milit involvement does not go much further than this. Actually, in C Rica, which has no army as such, and only a small national po one can hardly speak even of this minimal a military involvem

The four countries mentioned occupy an extreme position at one ıd of the spectrum of civil-military relations. At the other end can : found those countries which are more or less perpetual dictator-.ips, whether the armed force on which their governments rest is .at of the regular army (Paraguay), a party militia (Cuba), or an sortment of irregular para-military formations (Haiti). Most of e Latin American countries occupy the intermediate positions on e spectrum: the army interferes in politics, vetoes government ›licies, and on occasion removes the civilian government alto-:ther, without being invariably or exclusively in control.

In the distribution of the types of civil-military relations which ›tain in Latin America there seems an irregular, inconsistent, but :vertheless discernible tendency for countries to move from more less military influence in politics. Military governments hold ections and turn over control to civilians more frequently; longer :riods go by between military interventions. Political development ems to be taking place.

Intermittent Military Intervention. In the broad middle range of .e spectrum of military involvement in politics in Latin America, ırious types of military political behavior are found, ranging from mple pressure-group activity to open military rule. The distinguish-g characteristic of countries in this range, however, is that *both* .e military and organized civilian groups can be key factors in the ›litical process. Neither military supremacy—as in Paraguay—nor vilian supremacy—as in Uruguay—is assured. In this middle range .n thus be found those states in an intermediate stage of political :velopment.

Military intervention in politics needs to be understood not only terms of degree, but also in terms of motive. In Central America ıd the Caribbean, with the Dominican Republic the most blatant .se, the political activity of military officers is frequently designed mply to protect their opportunities to take graft. One of the rea-ns Juan Bosch was overthrown in 1963 was simply that he was :eping a close watch on what happened to public funds. In South merica, this type of behavior is less frequent, and military intervention is usually grounded on motives of policy. In such cases t military typically work together with disgruntled civilian grou which may on occasion even drag a reluctant military along in intervening.

It should not be overlooked, of course, that the military may pl the role of "guardians of the constitution," and intervene to remo dictators as well as democrats; a prodemocratic *coup* is possible.

It remains true, however, that the presumption should always against the military *coup d'état.* It represents a violation of legali sets a bad precedent, and induces or strengthens an unhealthy a unprofessional attitude among the soldiers. Even a *coup* staged wi the purpose of restoring the country to democracy needs to be ey askance; the military can be quite naive about politics, and m have misjudged the character of the incumbent regime by misund standing the alternatives available to it. Then, too, the members the new regime may prove incompetent, or worse, and the res may be a worse government or a more repressive dictatorship th the one that was overthrown; or the *coup* may begin a period continuing turmoil, as the successful conspirators fight amon themselves for supremacy.

After the military overthrow of a tyrant, the true "guardian the constitution" rules only provisionally until the heritage of t dictatorship can be liquidated, political life revived, orderly electio held, and the country returned to civilian authority. That has inde occurred at the political demise of Rojas Pinilla, Pérez Jiménez, a Perón, and it would be difficult to contend that General Arambu or Admiral Rojas, say, who were in the leadership of the rev against Perón, had acted other than honorably.

It has occurred, of course, that after a dictator has been ov thrown in a military *coup,* popular adulation has gone to the head the general who delivered the crucial ultimatum, and he has decid to hold on to power himself, rather than return it to civilian har at the earliest opportunity. This seems the most plausible expla tion for the actions of Rojas Pinilla of Colombia, who origina earned the people's gratitude by his overthrow of the tyranni ureano Gómez, only to earn their later opprobrium by his own nduct in office. In this case Rojas Pinilla overstepped the bounds the role of "guardian of the institution," became himself a dicor continuing in office by force and fraud, and must be judged ordingly.

The military in Brazil have traditionally assumed the role—often nsciously and explicitly—of "guardians of the constitution." Perps the army has felt responsible for the republican constitution, ce it was the army that forced Dom Pedro II to abdicate in 1889, ought the republic into existence, and provided its first President Deodoro da Fonseca. It was the armed forces, again, that escorted túlio Vargas from his dictatorial Presidency in 1945. In recent rs, the Brazilian army's distinctive conception of its constitutional e has resulted in some curious involvements on its part in the rmishing around the President's chair.

n 1955, for example, Marshal Lott's famous "preventive" *coup tat* occurred. The candidates on the winning ticket in the Presintial elections of that year, Juscelino Kubitschek and João Goulart, re strongly opposed by some Army leaders as too Leftist, and a *ıp* that would forestall their inauguration was in the making. é Café Filho, who had become President on the suicide of the umbent, again Getúlio Vargas, resigned; the then Acting Presint, Carlos Luz, dismissed Marshal Henrique Teixeira Lott from post as Minister of War to smooth the path of the projected *ıp*. Lott, for his part, staged a counter-*coup*, dismissed Luz, and, uratively speaking, presided over the ceremonies that inaugurated bitschek and Goulart. Lott's action thus constitutes the classic mple of the paradox of a *coup d'état* that protects the constiion.

A parallel situation in many respects was created at the resignan of the President who succeeded Kubitschek, Jânio Quadros, in gust of 1961. The chiefs of the armed services tried to bring ssure to prevent the accession to the Presidency of Goulart, who d been re-elected Vice-President. Lott, now a private citizen (he d run for the Presidency unsuccessfully against Quadros), taking a position similar to the one he had adopted six years before, v jailed for denouncing the maneuver, which eventually failed in face of popular opposition, the refusal of some key subordinate m tary commanders to follow the lead of the service chiefs, and mobilization for civil war of Goulart's home state of Rio Grande Sul. On this occasion it was their subordinates, and not the milit chiefs, who successfully defended constitutional norms by disob ing orders.

Four years later, the anti-Goulart forces moved again, with br civilian support, removing Goulart from the presidency, ostensi to prevent his perpetuating himself in power through constitutio amendment and the enfranchisement of illiterates, but also to fo stall the revolutionary social changes that were likely to follc military officers were especially incensed at Goulart's attempts to dermine the control of officers over their troops by his encoura ment of political activity by enlisted men. After the revolt of 19 however, the military themselves retained control, forsaking traditional role of "guardians of the constitution" and institut outright military rule under Marshal Humberto Castelo Branco a his successor after rigged elections, General Arturo Costa e Si

The Ecuadorean army has followed a parallel line of devel ment, at least for a short period. Playing the role of "guardian the constitution," it removed perennial president José María Vela Ibarra in 1935, 1947, and 1961, when he overstepped constitutio bounds, as it did with President Carlos Arroyo del Río in 19 When Velasco functioned more or less within the constitution was allowed to serve out his term peacefully (1952-56), howe as were Presidents Galo Plaza Lasso (1948-52) and Camilo Po Enríquez (1956-60). After the overthrow of President Arosem Monroy in 1963, however, the military junta that took office accep the view of one of its members, Colonel Marcos Gándara, that duty would not be fulfilled if it returned the country to civi hands in the same condition as it was taken over, but should f implement long overdue structural changes that would put the tional economy and governmental organization itself on a r nd more rational basis. Although the junta at first enjoyed wide-nging civilian support, it gradually alienated one political element ter another by its lack of comprehension of the complexities of the sks it had assumed, together with the heavy-handedness of its eatment of critics. The junta's unpopularity became so great that ss than three years after its assumption of power it was forced to sign and give way to a civilian provisional president without ing able to put up the slightest resistance.

Thus although the motives of a military group which perceives itself as playing the role of "guardian of the constitution" may more commendable than if they were purely self-interested, this eed not alter the outcome of the political situation, nor the quality the military performance in office.

To recapitulate, then: in the "middle range" of civil-military re-tions, between the extremes of continuing constitutional civilian le and continuing military rule, a variety of types of behavior co-xist. The military use influence and pressure on the head of govern-ent, perhaps vetoing measures of which they disapprove; and they ay intervene to remove the president altogether. In a situation like is, the president is figuratively always looking over his shoulder to bserve the reactions of military leaders to his policies, especially here the government must rely on the army to defend it against olent evidences of civilian dissatisfaction. But the military are emselves divided internally over political questions; and military overnments, too, can be forced to resign under pressure.

Continuing Military Rule. In several countries of Latin America, e country's politics are played out, at the highest level, among ilitary factions, and members of the armed forces openly occupy e leading positions on a continuing basis, without effective chal-nge from civilians. Although elections take place, the officer spon-red by the incumbent administration wins, with at most only ominal opposition. The military in power may be relatively well-tentioned and progressive, as in El Salvador, or relatively corrupt nd dictatorial, as in Paraguay; but in either case, it is the soldiers ho rule.

Pure military rule is most commonly found in the small tropica countries of the area—Paraguay, and the Central American an Caribbean republics—and is attributable in a general way to the lac of political maturity and the generally rudimentary stage of socia and political development reached in those republics. The distinctive characteristics of the "pure" military dictatorship are normall that the President is one of the army's ranking generals and hold the Presidential office by virtue of his military standing; that th support of no civilian political group is committed to him personally; and that he shares the power of political decision wit other senior officers.

From this position of chief military representative, of trustee o power for the army, the military dictator may build up his *persona* power, outmaneuver his military colleagues, and emerge as a personal dictator. This was especially easy for Rafael Trujillo in th Dominican Republic and Anastasio Somoza in Nicaragua, eac being the first commanding general of his country's newly reorganized and re-trained armed forces when the occupation of his countr by the U. S. Marines was liquidated. The personal nature of th rule that each enjoyed for over a generation was clearly illustrate by the striking parallels in the way the career of each was ended each was removed only by assassination, Somoza in 1956, Trujill in 1961, and in both cases the reins of power devolved (in the Trujillo case, only briefly) upon the dictator's son and namesake, wh held the rank of Commander-in-Chief. This situation is not a uncommon one: the dictator originally comes to power as corporat representative of the armed forces, but uses his position to establis a personal dictatorship.

The Personal Military Dictator. The final distinct type of militar involvement in politics, then, is that involving a personal dictato who springs from the military, but who may not have come t office by virtue of his rank, nor does he rely on the army as hi exclusive base of power. In fact, he erects a dictatorship *over* th army, alienating substantial groups within it, which may at the en cause his downfall.

The classic exemplar of this type in recent years is Juan D. Perón, ıe dictator of Argentina from 1945 to 1955. Marcos Pérez Jiménez f Venezuela (1953-59) and Batista of Cuba are also recent figures ı this category. Perón and Pérez Jiménez were both colonels when ıey started their respective rises to power; the strength of each lay ot in his position in the rank list, but in his leadership of a secret dge of "revolutionary" officers. For his part, Batista vaulted to ower originally from the lowly rank of sergeant with the aid of a rt of secret fraternity of N.C.O.'s. Neither Perón nor Pérez Jiméez assumed power immediately after the revolts in which they had ayed a major role, but each spent some time in a nominally subdinate role, consolidating his power before emerging openly as ıe regime's Presidential candidate. Similarly, Batista waited seven ars (1933-40) before running for President, during which time he ercised his power from behind the scenes.

Perón was highly successful in building support outside the army, rticularly among the labor unions, many of which he organized, ıd whose interests he was assiduous in promoting. He had never ıjoyed the united support of the officer corps, and his cultivation working-class support alienated segments of the military hierchy even more. Perón also made deliberate attempts to attract the pport of other distinct interests in the population—for example, his initial bid for the allegiance of the devout through the introıction of religious instruction in the schools.

Batista, during his first period in power (he went out of office in 44, returning by virtue of a *coup d'état* in 1952), and especially ıring his period in the Presidency, likewise managed to amass pular support, also primarily in the ranks of unionized labor. lthough Pérez Jiménez attempted to win favor among civilian oups during the early stages of his regime, his efforts always oved abortive, especially after the monstrous corruption that the ssession of power worked in him had begun to appear.

We will have further occasion to discuss the political techniques Perón, and comparable figures, in the sections on parties and the esidency.

CURBING THE POWER OF THE ARMY

The definitive establishment of a stable democratic regime nece sarily means the strict subordination of military to civilian authorit and the elimination of military initiatives from politics. This is course a task of colossal difficulty. It has been faced not only democratic governments in search of stability, but also by dictatc ships trying to free themselves from exclusive dependence on mi tary support.

One drastic method of eliminating the army as a political for is simply to defeat it in combat and disband it forcibly. This is effect what has happened, although in quite different contexts, the outcome of recent civil wars in Costa Rica in 1948, in Boliv in 1952, and in Cuba in 1957-58. In 1948 José Figueres raised t standard of revolt against the government's attempt to impose its ov choice as President in contravention of the results of the elections. the ensuing fighting Figueres's movement was successful and in co sequence the Costa Rican army, never very large or significant, w abolished entirely, the only armed force remaining being the nation police, whose numbers and armament are held to a minimum lev consistent with the routine preservation of domestic peace. In Boliv after 1952 and in Cuba after 1959, the victorious revolutionary mov ments disbanded the preexisting military forces, replacing them wi armies loyal to the revolution and supplementary militia forces. Bolivia the ruling MNR group was finally overthrown by its ov army after President Paz Estenssoro had alienated much of his su port by his policies and dictatorial conduct. In Cuba, Fidel Cast has taken care to base his political control not on his Rebel Arm which has been assigned to engineering and construction tasks, b on a popular militia and a network of committees of party activis who maintain close surveillance of the population.

The formation of a party militia to counterbalance an existi regular army is a delicate operation. President Villeda Morales Honduras was overthrown in 1963 partly because the army fear the competition of the militia he was building up. Similarly, t ill-fated government of Jacobo Arbenz Guzmán in Guatemala (1950-53) owed its demise in part to the fact that it was trying to create and arm a militia to forestall its overthrow at some future date by the leadership of the regular army, which was growing restive as a result of the government's far-reaching reform measures. The army refused to train and arm the militia, and Arbenz began to import arms from Eastern Europe, to the chagrin of the United States government; when the country was invaded by a small exile force under Castillo Armas (reputedly with the covert support of the United States' Central Intelligence Agency), the army refused to defend the regime and Arbenz was forced to relinquish his post.

The loyalty of a workers' militia, the "labor battalions" of Mexico City, on the other hand, was partly responsible for the survival of the Obregón government in Mexico in the face of the de la Huerta revolt of 1923. Probably the greater part of the army had gone over to the rebels, but the forces remaining loyal were buttressed by armed workers and the support of peasants who had received land, or anticipated doing so, under the government's agrarian reform program. This was the last revolt in Mexico that had a reasonable chance of succeeding, and marks the watershed, in Mexican history, between an era of turmoil and one of increasing stability. It was only due to the support of what was actually a kind of rudimentary workers' militia, too, that Perón managed to outlast army challenges to his rule, although eventually the armed forces were successful in removing him from office.

In principle, it should also be possible to limit the involvement of the armed forces in politics by playing "divide and rule" among the several armed services. There are some partial examples of use of this technique, without however substantial evidences of success. In most of the Latin American countries, of course, the army is by far the major armed service, and usually the only one in a position to play a significant political role. Chile's unusual geography, which gives her 2600 miles of coastline to only 296,000 square miles of territory, has made her navy the principal military arm. In fact, in the Chilean civil war of 1891, the Congress, supported by the navy, defeated President Balmaceda, who had the army fighting for him Argentina and Brazil also have substantial naval forces, and officers of the Argentine Navy were prominent in the opposition to Perón. Admiral Isaac Rojas serving as Vice-President in both provisional governments following Perón's ouster. In fact, the *coup de grâce* was administered to Perón by the navy's threat to bombard Buenos Aires unless he resign. Some elements in the Venezuelan navy (as well as in the air force) took a hand in the movement that culminated in the overthrow of Pérez Jiménez, and an admiral, Wolfgang Larrazábal, became Provisional President of the caretaker government.

There are commonly differences in political orientation among the leadership of the different armed services; in general, one can say that the officer corps of the Latin American navies tend to have more democratic leanings than do the officers of the armies of the area. Of course, naval forces are not put in the position of performing internal policing duties, so do not have the army's corporate interest in the preservation of internal order. In addition, the foreign naval training missions in the area have long been those of the United States; naval officers often go to the United States itself fo part of their training, and their professional models are the service of the United States and Great Britain. The training of some of the senior army officers, on the other hand, still goes back to the days in which German military missions and officers' schools wer popular.[7] Doubtless, a certain amount of ideology was imbibed along with the professional training.

In recent years, the new air forces in the area have begun to pla a political role. The Dominican air force, for example, which ha been built up considerably during the Trujillo dictatorship, took key part in the maneuvering that followed the assassination of th

[7] A German general served as chief of the Chilean General staff before an after the civil war of 1891, and the Bolivian army in the Chaco Wa (1933-38) was commanded, in the initial stages, by a German officer.

ctator, the ranking air force general becoming for a time Armed orces Commander-in-Chief. The air force of Ecuador played a key le in forcing the acceptance of Vice-President Carlos Julio Arosemena Monroy as President after the deposition of President Velasco arra in the fall of 1961, by attacking the Congressional chambers, here Arosemena was being held prisoner.

Although such incidents provide evidence that the navy and the force may be able to bring power to bear in a political showdown, r normal political purposes they remain imperfect political instruents by comparison with the army.

A technique for insuring against hostile military intervention hich has been tried without apparent success in Latin America lthough it may have helped Hitler, who used it), is to attempt to in a subjective commitment to the regime from the military by quiring the oath of allegiance to be taken to the dictator pernally, rather than to the fatherland; and by giving compulsory urses of indoctrination in the ideology of the regime. Perón may ve strengthened his position among the enlisted men in this shion, although the opposition of naval officers to his regime was doubtedly heightened by aversion to the personal oath and the doctrination sessions required of them. The armed forces of democcies also have their oaths of allegiance and their indoctrination ograms, of course, likewise of dubious efficacy.

Finally, there are administrative techniques of attempting to forell military intervention in politics, which governments of Mexico nce the Revolution have developed to a fine art. There is the freuent rotation of commands, so that a disgruntled general will not able to gain sufficient control over his subordinates, nor establh relations of confidence with them adequate to lead them into a bversive enterprise. Promotion lists can be screened, of course, so at the loyal are rewarded and the potentially disloyal retired from e service prematurely. If the would-be conspirator has already come too strong to separate from the service directly, then, dending on his rank, he can be posted abroad as military attaché to Embassy, sent around the world on some superfluous mission, or "promoted" to a seat in the cabinet at the head of one of the nc military departments, to remove him from a position of milit command, isolate him from his followers, and gain time to prep his downfall. An unscrupulous government can deliberately thr opportunities for large-scale graft in his way, in addition, either take the bite out of his dissatisfaction with the *status quo,* or alt natively so as to able to expose him subsequently and discredit h with civilian "good government" elements.

THE TYPES OF POLITICAL VIOLENCE

Discussions of politics normally confine themselves to the polit of stability: the maneuverings that occur when all sides accept t political institutions existing and work within and around them peaceful means. In Latin America, perhaps because there exists "legitimacy vacuum" of the type discussed above, politics frequen spills over the bounds of legality and operates outside them, taki the forms of what we might call a "politics of violence." The prese section will discuss this type of politics.

Some possible techniques of eliminating the military from poli cal activity were just discussed. Techniques of this type are a plicable, by and large, when the military is in politics because *wants* to be. It may also be the case, however, that circumstanc draw the army into the political arena, whether it wants to be the or not. If this is in fact the situation, then it is pointless to try neutralize the army by piecemeal techniques.

The army is necessarily involved in politics where there is standing expectation of violence and where the use of violence frequent and must be anticipated. Under these circumstances—f example, during the recent presidential terms of Rómulo Betanco in Venezuela and Arturo Frondizi in Argentina, where the life each of the two governments had been threatened by violence, the average, every other month—then the government needs co tinually to depend on the army to keep itself in power by crushi the attempts against it. The army, for its part, finds itself bei used as a political tool to maintain a government in office by su ressing the opposition; it finds itself acting against some political roups on behalf of others; and the senior officers inevitably ask ıemselves if this is the role they wish to play. They may decide, ; they have decided in Venezuela up to the time of writing, that is their duty to support the incumbent constitutional government; ut the temptation to stipulate conditions for their continued support will prove virtually irresistible, and the army will come to play ıe role described above as that of the "veto group." In other words, ıe government is put under the constraint of having to consider ıe views of the senior military leaders, and often of modifying olicy consistent with their wishes, either expressed or anticipated.

On the other hand, an army that is being used to maintain a egime in power may rebel against the use to which it is being put, nd either turn out the government itself,[8] or, like the Guatemalan rmy at the time of the Castillo Armas invasion against the Arbenz overnment described above, assume a "neutral" position and allow ıe government to be overthrown.

It should not be assumed, from the foregoing discussion, that the rmed forces always hold the key to the outcome of situations of onflict—nor, for that matter, that all resorts to violence entail the se of organized military force as such. For purposes of clarity, let s posit the existence of a continuum of types of political action anging from the peaceful and law-abiding expression of opinion in public speech, say, all the way to civil war to the death. Then, nany forms of political action only part of the way along the scale re common in the political life of Latin America, and in fact the verwhelming proportion of uses of force for political purposes are ess than total. Let us review the most common types of "direct ction," action outside constitutional channels, proceeding from the ess to the more violent ends of the scale.[9]

[8] Colonel Nasser, in his book *The Philosophy of the Revolution,* explains the gyptian army's overthrow of the monarchy in these terms.

[9] The creation of a single scale here is an unfortunately unavoidable overimplification, of course. Here, as in other sections of the book, the author is ndebted to the perceptive writings of Professor Kalman H. Silvert.

At the head of the direct action scale, one would have to set (1) *the mere threat of violence,* which may achieve the intended effect by itself. This may consist of no more than a statement of disapproval, public or private, of a given policy, say, together with the hint that, if necessary, disapproval may take a more concrete form. For example, the ranking general may announce something like "The armed forces direct me to express the gravest doubts about the wisdom of the policy with respect to *x* followed by His Excellency the Constitutional President of the Republic, and feel constrained to make clear that in the event of widespread public disorders attendant upon the final adoption of that policy, the armed forces cannot answer for the safety of the government"—the latter part of the statement being a hint that the army will connive at a *coup d'état* if need be. Or, of course, the threat may be more open and direct.

Different varieties of what are called in Latin America (2) *manifestaciones,* public demonstrations, rallies, parades, and the like, constitute a further stage along the road of violence, although a wide range of types of activity can be grouped under this head. Such demonstrations may pass off without further incident—everyone may go home quietly after the speeches are made, the slogans shouted, and enthusiasm for the cause built up. The justification for calling a peaceful demonstration of this kind a form of violent direct action is that the intended result is generally that of a show of strength—in effect, a kind of threat, as much as if to say: "Here we are, numerous, well-disciplined, enthusiastic; today we merely assemble peacefully; but if you do not adopt the policy we urge, we may not be so peaceable next time."

Of course, demonstrations frequently do not end without further incident, but develop instead into (3) *isolated acts of violence.* Buses and cars are stopped, overturned, smashed, burned; the houses and shops of members of opposing groups are stoned, broken into, looted. The forces entrusted with the maintenance of public order, for their part, are not standing idly by, and the forcible dis ersal of public demonstrations of opposition forces is extremely ommon in Latin America—especially, of course, when the crowd ecomes a violent mob and heads for the Presidential Palace; but ot infrequently when the demonstration has been perfectly peace-le. Many dictatorships could find the turning-point in the train f events that led to their downfall in the public indignation follow-g the death of some participant in a peaceful demonstration on hich the police had opened fire. Actually, in several of the repub-cs the police force in the capital includes riot squads trained and quipped for the dispersal of crowds without the use of firearms—ith waterhoses, for example, or by tear gas; but all too often lives e lost unnecessarily—and with adverse political repercussions—by cess of zeal, or more likely of nervousness, on the part of the lice.

(4) *The strike* should also be listed here, because it commonly as political aims, in contrast to its normal limited use for economic irposes in the United States. Its use becomes political, in Latin merica, even where its goals are those of improvements in wages, ours, or conditions of work, because government intervention in bor disputes is so widespread, and so expected, that the desired itcome of a labor dispute will entail favorable government action any case. In addition, unions also regularly use the strike weapon influence government policy on questions other than those di-ctly relating to labor.

On the other hand, the use of the strike for political ends has read to groups other than organized labor. A strike by shopkeepers Port-au-Prince in 1956 forced President Magloire from office, for ample; a strike of professional men and women occasioned the wnfall of Carlos Ibáñez del Campo, the dictator of Chile, in 1931; d a physicians' strike forced the resignation of the Salvadorean ctator Hernández Martínez in 1944.

Sporadic and isolated acts of violence were discussed above in nnection with political demonstrations. Different in kind from em are the systematically planned individual acts of violence that go by the name of (5) *terrorism.* A terrorist campaign of assassina-tions and bombings, like the other types of act described above, ma have the intention of directly inducing either a change in policy, c a change in government. It may also have the same effect indirectl however, in that by forcing the government to become increasing repressive in the all but impossible attempt to end terrorist attack it brings indifferent or apathetic public opinion increasingly over the opposition. This was certainly the effect, probably intended, the decision by Fidel Castro's movement to use terrorist tacti against the Batista dictatorship, which had until that time been rel tively mild compared with what it later became, and which ha been tolerated by large segments of the public that were rapid alienated as the regime became more and more repressive in r sponse to the *fidelista* campaign of terror.

Directly and immediately aiming at a change in government, course, is the (6) *golpe,*[10] the forcible removal of the top politic leadership from the seats of power, and their replacement by th leaders of the revolt. The classical Latin American "revolution" of this uncomplicated type, and still occurs in this form, especial in the smaller countries, though no longer so frequently as formerl Typically, the "palace revolt" of this type is engineered by a segme of the upper levels of command in the armed forces, involves litt or no actual fighting, and is heard of by the public for the fir time when the leadership of the revolt, now the "Provisional Go ernment" or the "Patriotic Junta," announces the change over th radio and urges the citizens to remain calm and go about their no mal business. Under the etiquette of the old-style *golpe,* the ou going President and his colleagues would be permitted to go in exile, their departure facilitated and escorted. The extent of th military action accompanying the *coup* would be the deployme of a couple of platoons of men around the Presidential Palace, pe haps the Legislative Palace, and probably the radio stations (to pr vent loyalists from broadcasting an appeal for support). If the *cou* is properly prepared, and the element of surprise preserved, th

[10] In English, *coup d'état!*

President has no opportunity to do anything else but yield, and relinquish his post.

In the case of what we may call the (7) *pronunciamento,* more people are involved, the power play occurs in public view, and the incumbent President has alternative actions among which he may choose. In a *pronunciamento,* a body of people—a section of the armed forces, a party, the people of a state or province—"pronounce" against the regime; that is, they openly raise the standard of revolt. After this has occurred, various consequences are possible: the rebels may march on the capital, gathering support on the way, there or near there to fight a decisive pitched battle against the adherents of the regime. The incumbents, on the other hand, may take a quick survey of the strength of the forces aligned on either side, and decide to retire into exile without pressing the issue to a trial of arms; perhaps all that is necessary is to sound out the leadership of the armed forces to determine whether it is prepared to fight the rebels or not, in order for the President to gauge which alternative to choose. And so it may be sufficient for an opposition leader to "pronounce" against the government, and then sit back and wait for it to fall.

Of course, the result may equally well go against him; those he thought would follow him in "pronouncing" may instead protest their loyalty; the armed forces may prepare to take to the field; and he may have to go into exile himself, or face capture and imprisonment. The *pronunciamento,* then, can eventuate in different ways —in a transfer of power attended with hardly more violence or public disturbance than the tradition *golpe;* or in protracted fighting that develops into actual (8) *civil war.*

A revolt of the *pronunciamento* type originating with a single barracks is known as the *cuartelazo* (*cuartel* = barracks). This may approach very close to the *golpe,* in that the showdown may occur entirely within the military, civilians playing only the role of bystanders, while the transfer of power takes place speedily and the action is localized. On the other hand, it clearly differs from the *golpe* in that the revolt occurs outside the circle of those having immediate access to the President, who is then left with a choice o alternative actions, to resist or not; while the rebels are prepare to fight if necessary.

MEETING THE THREAT OF VIOLENCE

What should be noted about the uses of violence referred to abov is that it may be sufficient, and usually will be, merely to posses force and be prepared to use it; the necessity of actually sheddin blood need not arise. The adversary may calculate the relativ strengths of the two sides and decide to yield without bringing th issue to a hopeless trial of strength. Or he may not have the nerve or the stomach, or the indifference to the loss of life, necessary t settle the contest by violence. This means, in effect, that a showdow over the control of the government or even over the direction o policy, where the threat of the use of force is involved, is in part contest of wills. That is, an advantage lies with the more determine adversary—the one who is the more prepared to raise the level o violence. The adversary who shrinks from the use of violence is a a disadvantage in the struggle; he will be under pressure to yiel rather than stand his ground and prepare for a physical conflict In other words, the threat to use force may prove, where countere by an opposing willingness to use force, no more than a bluff.

Of course it takes courage, and a confidence in the eventual out come of the dispute, to call a bluff of this kind. One reason to hav confidence in a favorable outcome is the assurance of preponderan popular support; so that if the issue were to be pushed even to th point of civil war, the balance of forces would be favorable. Con versely, a bluff is more likely to collapse when the bluffer can b confronted with the threat to expand the theatre of conflict, an realizes that if this happens, his forces will be defeated by th opposition of the masses of the people.

One meaning of the foregoing is that a determined civilian gov ernment that has popular support can defy a military ultimatur to resign. That is, since it is possible for a popular cause to defea a regular army in civil war—it has been done, as was mentione bove, in Cuba, Bolivia, and Costa Rica, in recent years—the mili- ıry leaders may therefore be reluctant to follow through on an ltimatum that has been defied.

This occurred in Brazil during 1961, when the leaders of all three rmed services announced that they would not accept as President, ão Goulart, who as Vice-President was constitutionally entitled to ıcceed to the office from which Jânio Quadros had just resigned. Iowever, when they were made to realize by the steadfastness of the ioulart forces that their position could only be maintained by ıe successful prosecution of a civil war, the military leaders re- eated and accepted the inauguration of Goulart. Of course, all ıree military ministers were subsequently retired from the service y President Goulart. It had been made clear that the forces favor- ıg the inauguration of Goulart would not accept the ultimatum f Marshal Denys and the other senior military leaders in several 'ays: some subordinate commanders announced that thenceforth ıey would take orders only from Goulart as constitutional Presi- ent; one after another, leading political figures announced their lherence to the principles of succession provided in the constitu- on; and the governor of Goulart's home state of Rio Grande do ul (who happened also to be Goulart's brother-in-law) mobilized is supporters in the state in preparation for civil war—an action :miniscent of the *pronunciamento* that originally brought Getúlio 'argas to the Presidency 31 years before. (By 1964, however, the ılance of power had shifted enough for Goulart to be overthrown a revolt of the *pronunciamento* variety.)

Given circumstances of this type, there are several reasons why ıe leaders of an army enjoying an apparent position of prepon- :rant strength may back down on an ultimatum they have given ther than carry it through, where that means actual fighting. As a ıle, armies prefer to avoid fighting in any case; especially so when ıis involves fighting against compatriots. This reluctance will be rengthened, on the part of the army leadership, by the fact that though they have spoken in the name of the entire army in their olitical intervention, in actuality many subordinate commanders would not be prepared to follow their lead into combat against th legally constituted civilian authorities. In an actual trial of strengt the political generals at the top can guess that they will not be abl to count on the continued loyalty to them of lower-ranking office actually commanding troops. And yet even if the chain of comman holds, and the army *in toto* takes to the field against organize civilian groups supporting the government, a popular governme can count on widespread desertion among the enlisted men, relu tant to fire on friends and neighbors fighting in a cause with whic they probably sympathize. This possibility, too, must be present i the mind of the general preparing to force his will on a recalcitra government.

And so popular support itself constitutes a reservoir of strengt on which a government can draw to withstand a military threa A particularly striking demonstration of this thesis is given by th history of the development of stability in the government of Mexic over the last 40 years.

Until Porfirio Díaz had instituted his iron dictatorship in the la quarter of the nineteenth century, Mexican political history had ru in the stereotyped channels of successful insurrection, dictatorshi crisis over succession to the Presidency, and further insurrectio After Díaz was overthrown by the Revolution of 1910, it seemed if the old pattern would be revived. Venustiano Carranza manage to impose his authority over the other Revolutionary leaders an make himself President, only to be confronted, toward the end his term, with a succession crisis and a successful revolt led by th man who felt he should have been picked as the government's Pres dential candidate, but had not been: Álvaro Obregón. In class fashion,[11] when Obregón's choice to succeed himself as Preside became known (it was Plutarco Elías Calles), the disappointed riv candidate, Adolfo de la Huerta, "pronounced" against the regin and began to gather an army.

According to all the precedents, the revolt was bound to succee

[11] The dynamics of the classic succession crisis are depicted masterfully Martin Luis Guzmán in his novel *La Sombra del Caudillo*.

eading Revolutionary generals went over to the revolt, being joined n insurrection by probably the greater part of the army. In the ast, the people had almost automatically sided with the "outs" on he premise that things couldn't get worse and might even get better. But this revolt was different. The difference was that this time the eople had something to lose if the revolt succeeded; during his erm Obregón had fostered union organization and promoted social egislation, as well as starting to implement the Revolution's program of land reform. Not only did this revolt collapse, but subsequent "election time" revolts became progressively feebler until by 940 the defeated candidate fulminated and threatened, but refrained rom raising the standard of revolt. Since then Presidential elections ave no longer meant civil war in Mexico. This atrophy of the habit f revolution is directly traceable to the reform measures which nsured that, on the whole, the major organized interests of the ountry would have an interest in the preservation of the *status quo* hat would lead them to fight, if need be, on the side of the contitutional authorities. In this sense one can say that, given the existnce of military disaffection, the best guarantee of continuance in ffice is broad popular support.

RUE REVOLUTIONS

Perhaps at this juncture one should pause to make the point—*le rigeur* in studies of Latin American politics—that the violent hanges of political control which occur so frequently in the region nd generally pass for revolutions, can hardly be called "revoluions" in the strict sense of an overturn of society and polity, since he changes that occur have often consisted of no more than the ubstitution of one group of individuals for another without fareaching consequences for the society. To earn the title of "revoluion," a shift in the locus of power should be more than a palace evolt with the ruling circle, or a *cuartelazo*. It is often said that the evolution proper involves a restructuring of society and politics, a e-shuffling of the class system. This is of course true, and in this ense there can be "peaceful revolutions," just as much as there can be violent shifts of power that are not revolutions. In fact, the genuine revolutionary process, the re-making of society, is likely to extend over a considerable period of time. In official parlance in Mexico, the Mexican Revolution that began in 1910 is regarded as still continuing.

Now the changes that collectively constitute the revolutionary process do not occur at random; they aim at fulfilling the goals of the revolution, at giving its ideals concrete embodiment in new institutions and patterns of behavior. If this is so, then the distinctive feature of a revolution is that it establishes new goals for the society; it reorganizes society, but it must first reorganize the values which that society accepts; a successful revolution means the acceptance as "good" of things that were not regarded as good before, the rejection as "bad" of things previously acceptable or commendable.

This transformation of the accepted value system can clearly be seen if one looks again at the example just cited above, the Mexican Revolution of 1910, one of the few genuine revolutions in Latin America. Prior to the Revolution, the Indian was semi-officially regarded as an inferior being, to be kept out of sight as much as possible, being prohibited by Porfirio Díaz's police from entering the Alameda, the public park in the center of Mexico City, for example. After the Revolution, Mexico's Indian heritage became a matter of national pride, to be stressed in her art and her history, to be studied at length in her universities, and the Indian himself became a subject of special government attention and expenditure. Prior to the Revolution, foreign investment was to be favored, nurtured, and protected, as one of the cardinal principles of national policy. After the Revolution, the presumption was to be against foreign investment, its role in the economy to be limited progressively to a demonstrably necessary minimum.

If the revolutionary process consists of the progressive implementation in practice of the new ideals posited by the revolution, then it is quite possible that not all the changes that occur will have been envisaged specifically by the original leadership. It is even true oreover, that the ideals that the revolution comes to have will not limited to those espoused by the original leaders of the revolu- on. In the revolutionary process, ideas which were "in the air," hich were ripe for official acceptance, which embody genuine pop- ar aspirations, will attach themselves to the ideology of the revo- tion, which in retrospect will have become something more than, though not opposed to, what the original leaders of the revolution ntemplated. The initiator of the Mexican Revolution, Francisco Madero, for example, limited his demands to political reform— Effective Suffrage; No Re-Election" in the motto that remains the icial slogan of the Revolution to this day—whereas in retrospect e major achievements of the Revolution include, as well as the litical reform, the reform of the landholding system, the estab- hment of unions, the incorporation of the Indian into national e, and the initiation of industrialization.

A clearer case, from our own day, of the autonomy of the revo- tionary process once started in motion is that of the Bolivian Revo- tion of 1952. Neither of the two major structural changes wrought the Revolution to date, the land reform and the nationalization the tin mines, was deliberately initiated by the leadership of the ational Revolutionary Movement that the revolution brought to wer, although both measures were quite in keeping with MNR ctrine. The peasants seized the land, and the tin workers seized e mines; the government was left to establish a basis of legality the *faits accomplis.*

One would probably be justified, accordingly, in concluding that e authentic revolutions that occur in Latin America in the present , although they may take place under a variety of auspices and hibit national peculiarities, if they are to succeed and establish emselves permanently, will embody the political values generally cepted today as legitimate: the legal equality of persons, the uni- rsal right to participate through representatives in political deci- n-making, and the individual's claim on his government for cial justice. Not all of the Latin American countries have political lers that recognize these principles in practice; by peaceful or violent means, revolutions that embody these principles will cor to them.

E. PARTIES AND PARTY SYSTEMS

THE DIMENSIONS OF PARTY

Politics is everywhere party politics. It is hard to imagine in wh way representative government could have any meaning withc political parties. Parties enable the voter to choose among intel gible alternatives. They develop and bring forward candidates fill offices in the gift of the people. At their best, they unite politi officials scattered among different branches of government in t concerted attempt to effect a political program.

Accordingly, parties can be described in terms of three maj characteristics: the party's program, and the general principles frc which that program purports to be derived, the party ideology; t social groups from which the party draws its electoral support, a those from which its leaders come; and, less important, the ch features of the internal organization of the party. The actions party leaders, however, will depend not only on these attribu peculiar to the individual party, but also on the environment which the party operates, the whole political system. Necessari this environment includes the whole range of factors discussed this book: political culture, social structure, and governmental str ture. But it includes in addition two factors that may especia appropriately be considered along with the parties themselves: pa systems, and electoral systems.

This section will deal, then, with the major factors, both trinsic and extrinsic, which together determine party acts, taki up first the combined dimension of ideology and social sources support.

PARTY TYPES, BY IDEOLOGY

In general, as one locates parties along a scale from Right to L from conservative to radical, from supporters of the *status quo* novators, one is also proceeding down the social ladder so far as e category into which the supporters of each party fall is con-rned. In other words, the more conservative the party, the more kely its supporters are to be of high social status. This is of course be expected, since those who resist change can be expected to be ose who have most to lose by change. The assumption here is that major determinant of political choice is the individual's class (that usually, economic) interest, and this is on the whole a sound as-mption. In actuality, the individual normally—where the same rties continue to exist over time—inherits his party affiliation in atin America just as in the United States; but he also inherits his ass status, so the two continue in harmony in the typical case.

The assumption that individual social and economic interest de-rmines party choice, although true in general, is not invariably lid; one could multiply examples of people who "should" sup-ort parties other than those they do. Nevertheless, the original as-mption is accurate enough to serve as the basis for the discussion the major varieties of party taken up in the following paragraphs. These varieties are treated as separate parties, although in some untries, depending on the nature of the party system, they may ist as tendencies within larger, more inclusive, parties, or alterna-vely as coalitions of splinter groups in a fragmented system. No ngle country has parties representing the entire range of political ndencies listed below, although Chile comes close.

The Conservatives. Traditional Conservative parties, under vari-is names, exist in perhaps half of the republics. They date, of urse, from the earliest days of Independence, and, in a sense, even rlier. Essentially, the Conservatives represent the highest-status oups, the social elite, reproducing at their core the alliance of rge landowners, high prelacy, and topmost echelon of military mmand that ruled during colonial times.

Today, however, members of families that still call themselves onservative or remain loyal to Conservative parties may be in-lved in modern business activities and no longer dependent on income from land ownership; their ideas may no longer be those appropriate to the *ancien régime*. In fact, Latin American Conserv tives, faced with the challenges of the modern world, have react in three different ways: probably the major part of Conservatis chooses to stand pat in its traditional position, denying any necessi for change and steadily losing touch with political reality; a mo erate wing of Conservative thought has accepted the need to chan although attempting to control it, limit it, and slow it down, p serving as much as possible of the *status quo;* while a third segme has reacted violently, taking an extreme position and resorting force and fraud in the attempt to maintain the traditional soc order.

The central core of ideas of Latin American Conservatism m fairly be summarized as follows. Society inevitably includes clas of people of different abilities, sensibilities, and merit. People in t lower classes (especially where they are predominantly Indian) ha baser feelings, could not appreciate the refinements of living joyed by the upper classes, and would not work unless their co dition made it absolutely necessary. Society requires order, w each abiding in his proper place: a doctrine properly taught by t Church, which should be especially protected and encouraged the State, especially in its ministry to the lower classes. The soc order that should be maintained includes the present distributi of property. Proposals involving the redistribution of property, su as progressive taxation or land reform, are clearly inspired by int national Communism and would destroy the fabric of organized ciety, challenge the Divine order in the world, and tend to t obliteration of proper social distinctions. In any case, attempts social amelioration are doomed by the fact that the harsh realit of life are unavoidable features of the human condition, which w not yield to human exertions.

With views of this kind, it is evident that traditional Conser tive parties can accept democracy only half-heartedly or with res vations, if at all. In fact, several Conservative parties have lo established reputations as falsifiers of elections, this being often only method by which a Conservative party can win elections age of democracy. Rigging elections was the policy of Argentine ıservatives until 1910 and then again from 1930 to 1942, and the .ombian Conservatives have been guilty of the same thing. The mples from Central America are legion, of course.

'or similar reasons, some Conservative politicians have cooperated h military leaders in staging anti-democratic *coups*.

Jormally, Conservative chances in honest national elections de-d on the discovery of a charismatic personality who can win *oite* his identification with the party; the fragmentation of the osition (thus Ponce Enríquez was elected Ecuadorean President 1956 from a field of three major candidates with only about 35 cent of the vote cast); or the formation of a coalition (for exam- in Chile the Conservative party has been able to join with erals and Radicals to form a majority combination).

. was mentioned above that, around the central core of Con-'ative belief, divergent tendencies exist. On the Right extreme, ıservatism shades into fascism—for example, in the politics of ıreano Gómez, the vitriolic Colombian newspaper publisher, ner President and dictator of his unhappy country. With Lau-ıo, Conservatism becomes reactionary, espousing violence against ersaries, bitterly hostile to the United States, Hispanophile (that ond of Spain), and pro-Franco. The regime of General Uriburu, ch took power in Argentina in 1930, also bore this general com-:ion.

everal minor political organizations outside the Conservative :ies—none of them having today a chance of coming to power ough peaceful means—must be identified as downright fascist. : major fascist movements of Latin America are—or were, since vogue of fascism has long passed its peak—the *Sinarquistas* of xico; the *Integralistas* in Brazil, led by Plinio Salgado, who at his ı point garnered 8% of the vote in a Presidential election; Gon-z von Marees' *Nacista* party in Chile, now defunct, although ıy former *Nacistas* are still active in Chilean politics; the *ARNE* Ecuador; and formerly, although perhaps no longer, the *Falange 'alista Boliviano*. In addition, many dictators in office have

organized parties which necessarily, because of their use of
ience, their exaltation of the leader, and their hostility to civil f
dom, have features that appear fascist; whether one calls these
ties fascist or not depends on how broad a definition he wishe
allow the term. As in all countries, the fascists of Latin America
the mentally unbalanced, the misfits of all classes, from top to
tom of the social scale. The avowed fascists, to repeat, are out
the Conservative fold, although they are often tolerated by C
servatives as people "who mean well, but go to extremes."

The moderate Conservatives—like the Ospinistas in Colombia
the followers of Manuel Prado in Peru—although sharing t
basic outlook on society with the other Conservative tendencies, t
the position that one must make concessions to the times—to b
to the wind lest one break, as it were. These Conservatives sup
constitutional government and accept democracy. They are on
whole pro-United States and sided with the Allies during W
War II (the Laureanista type of Conservative supported the A
as a rule). Most members of the *Partido de Acción Nacional*
Mexico would fall into this category, along with the *Pradistas*
Ospinistas already cited.

The recent political history of Nicaragua, Paraguay, and H
duras necessitates a special word about the Conservative partie
those countries. The major part of the Paraguayan Conserva
party, the Colorados,[12] has been simply an annex to the strong
military regime presided over by General Stroessner. The C
servatives of Honduras, the Nationalist party, stood in a sim
relationship to the dictatorship of Carías Andino, the wing of
party opposed to Carías subsequently becoming the *Movimie*
Reformista. In Nicaragua, on the other hand, it is the Natio
Liberal party that has been a utensil of the Somoza dictators
but the Conservatives, too, have split over the issue of collaborat
with the regime.

Liberals and Radicals. The emergence of the various parties

[12] Not to be confused with the Colorados in Uruguay.

scussed briefly as part of a retrospect on the development of politi- l issues in Latin America. As was pointed out, the original party uggle in the years following Independence in most of the repub- s was between Conservatives and Liberals. As more and more oups were admitted to participation in the political process— ways those a little further down the socioeconomic scale—new litical tendencies came into prominence, except for the fascist oups previously discussed always to the Left of the Liberal parties. countries where strong forces (to be discussed) made for the ntinuation of the two-party system, these tendencies were ab- rbed by, or contained within, the Liberal party. Where influences nducive to the maintenance of the two-party system were weak lacking, a multi-party system developed. The possible fates in re for the Liberal party, then, were the following: it could be- me, in time, the dominant party in a two-party system, containing thin itself various social groups and political tendencies. This is at has happened in Uruguay, Colombia, Honduras, and (until ently) Ecuador, where the Liberal parties include not only a ditional moderate wing, but also more radical elements like those erred to below as *aprista.* Alternatively, the Liberals could dis- pear from the scene, being absorbed into the newer parties or ing over to the Conservatives as the upper social groups coalesced ainst the newly emergent elements. Today, in fact, most of the publics have no Liberal party as such. Thirdly, the party could ntinue to exist, where conditions favored a multi-party system, t on the basis of a narrow range of support. This development s reached its maximum in Chile, where the Liberals are simply e of a half a dozen "major" parties. Support of the Liberal party Chile has narrowed down to comprise today principally moder- ly progressive businessmen and managers of the type of the cent President, Jorge Alessandri Rodríguez.

Traditionally, the Liberals have been open-minded toward change, ging the cause of individual freedom against the Conservatives' ampionship of the principle of order, and favoring the rights of parliament over executive prerogative and, usually, those of lo autonomy against central control. The Liberal is customarily least mildly anti-clerical.

The core of support for the traditional Liberal party came usua from groups which, while part of the social elite, were not p dominantly dependent on income from large estates, but were co nected with business and "progressive" professions—journalism, la and university teaching. The "inclusive" Liberal parties cited abo those operating in two-party systems, have today, in addition, wo ing-class support.

The Radical parties grew out of the Left side of the Liberals, it were, appealing especially to lawyers, schoolteachers, and ci servants, and stressing in their programs the extension of the s frage, honest elections, and anti-clericalism, the latter especially it applied to the schools, typical issues being those of governme aid to religious schools and religious instruction in public scho In Argentina, the Radicals absorbed the Liberals, emerging as eas the country's major party in numbers of supporters from 1910 c The party split in the 1920s and has again split in recent years. Af the overthrow of Perón in 1955 the party divided over the questi of what attitude to take towards the Peronists, with the strong ar Peronist line being taken at first by the People's Radicals (UCR under the leadership of Ricardo Balbín, and the milder, even c laborationist, tendency represented by Arturo Frondizi and t Intransigent Radicals (UCRI). Frondizi was subsequently elect President with the aid of Peronist votes; when he was overthrown the military for being "soft on Peronism" in 1962, the rump UC was left without a distinctive political position, while Frond organized his remaining followers into the MID (Movement f Integration and Development). Under the circumstances of politi fragmentation and the banning of the Peronists which then obtain the People's Radicals managed to elect their candidate, Arturo Ill to the Presidency in 1964. However, Illia was overthrown in tu as being allegedly ineffectual and also "soft on Peronism," 1966, and replaced by an outright military government under Ge

ıl Juan Carlos Ongania. Despite some tendencies in the direc-
n of the modernization of the People's Radicals during Illia's
esidency, the party is still widely regarded as an ineffective com-
ıation of old machine politicians with old-fashioned ideas.

The Radicals of Chile, the other country where the party still
ıys a major role, seem also in decline. Long accustomed, like
: French Radicals, to dominate the political system by virtue of
ɜir pivotal position, from which the party could make alliances
either the Right or the Left, the Chilean Radicals have been
;placed as the key party in the system by the rise of the Christian
:mocrats, who captured the Presidency in 1964. The Chilean
.dicals have still not found a new vocation; and their fate suggests
ıt Radicalism has been passed by the political tendencies of
lay, its leading ideas no longer relevant to today's problems, its
mer supporters finding more effective champions elsewhere.

:hristian Democrats or Christian Socialists. The growth of the
ıristian Democrats as a distinctive category of political party is
:dominantly a phenomenon of the period since the end of World
ar II. Christian Democracy, or Christian Socialism, as it is some-
ıes known, is an attempt to combine loyalty to the Church, and
ɔport of its political claims—which, while varying from country
country in relation to the number of the devout and the traditions
each land, always include autonomy for church schools and the
ɔtection of religious instruction and worship—with a progressive
ɜition on social questions. That is, traditionally, in Latin America
least as much as in Europe, support for the Church has been
ntified with social conservatism. The doctrines of the Church
ecting politics that were most emphasized were those elaborating
: duties of obedience to secular authorities, which must be pre-
ned to be ordained of God. Christian Democracy has chosen
her to stress those elements of Catholic doctrine that postulate
: duty of all to be charitable in mutual relations, to acknowledge
ɖ respect the spiritual equality and the familial needs of all
mankind. Specifically, this position finds its immediate authori-
ive support in the social encyclicals of Leo XIII (and now of

John XXIII) and especially the *Rerum Novarum* and *Quadreg simo Anno*, which, although not as "socialist" as often supposed, acknowledge the necessity for minimum standards of life for wor ingmen, and point out that capitalism in itself does not satisfy t requirements that Christianity demands of an economic system.

These views were not new in Catholic thought when announc authoritatively, of course, but the stress placed on them at the tir constituted something of a departure from pre-existing practice. Tl was still a long way from countenancing "Christian" politic parties, however, the position of the Church having normally be that it did not care to be identified exclusively, even indirectly, wi any single political current, but would maintain good relations wi all political tendencies that did not clearly violate Christian norr nor attack the necessary secular basis for religious worship and i struction. Accordingly, while small "Christian" political parties the Center and Center-Left were founded in the first three decad of the century, in Uruguay and Chile (as they were in Italy a France), these were barely tolerated by the Church hierarchy, a never gained the stature of major parties in the inter-war period.

Christians in politics were drawn to the Left, however, duri the period of fascist dominance in Europe, when they found the selves cooperating, in the opposition or underground, with Libera Socialists, and Communists. Something of the same effect was noti able a little later in Argentina, Peru, and Venezuela, where similar broad-based cooperation, in the open, underground, or in exile, w effected against the dictatorships of Perón (in its later stages), Odr and Pérez Jiménez, respectively. In the meantime the Church h relaxed and—almost, but not quite—abandoned its reservatio about "Christian Socialist" parties, and parties were founded in Pe and Argentina to join the now flourishing Christian Democra movements of Chile and Venezuela.

The status of the individual parties today is roughly as follov in Venezuela the Christian Social party (COPEI, after an earli name) is the second or third largest party in the country in the si of its support, and constitutes the major opposition to its form ırtner in the government coalition, *Acción Democrática*. In Chile, ːe Christian Democrats were able to win power on their own in a agmented political situation, electing Eduardo Frei president in ʻ64 and gaining an absolute majority in the Chamber of Deputies. he enactment of the party's reform program remained at first deːndent on securing support from the representatives of other parties the Senate, however. Frei aimed at the incorporation into full ırticipation in Chilean society, economy, and politics of urban slumvellers and landless rural workers, hitherto on the margins of naɔnal life because of their illiteracy and economic weakness; at rapid onomic growth; at land reform; and at the establishment of new lations with foreign investors that would be mutually satisfactory ıd profitable, while upholding Chile's national dignity. If the ːwly participant masses should vote Christian Democratic out of atitude to their benefactors, then the party could be assured of an definite tenure in office.

The election of Frei sent a surge of elation and hope through the hristian Democrats of the continent and helped create the wideread feeling that Christian Democracy is the movement that will herit the future. The parties denominated Christian Democratic or hristian Social are now of account in about half of the republics, erywhere attracting bright and vigorous younger intellectuals. The ırties of El Salvador, Panama, and perhaps the Dominican Reıblic seem destined for ultimate success, although the parties in rgentina, Bolivia, and Brazil have futures clouded by military tervention and the opportunistic behavior of party leaders. In Peru, e Christian Democrats, though few in number, have joined in alition with the personalist movement of Fernando Belaúnde, cción Popular, providing it not only with the critical margin of ɔtes that elected Belaúnde president in 1963, but also with many of e key figures and leading ideas of his government. The party may ıus have earned the right to inherit Belaúnde's following after he tires from the Presidency.

A problem faced by all the parties of Christian-Social orientation that of maintaining equilibrium between the terms at the two ends of the hyphen, as it were, and especially of not allowing t party's pro-clerical predilections to eclipse its stand for social pro ress. The problem arises in this form because many supporters a attracted to an avowedly Christian party, for reasons of conscienc who do not share its progressive orientation on social questions. T more devout are still likely, in Latin America as elsewhere, to the more conservative; and the party's leaders have to mainta constant vigilance lest the party's political position begin to dri Rightward in response to opinion among the rank and file. T Christian Democrats are particularly subject to the operation centrifugal ideological forces, since they draw support from all leve of society, and all walks of life: organized labor, business, the profe sions, and agriculture. To be a "Christian Democrat" sounds an feels more pleasant than to be a "Conservative," apparently, an moderate Conservative parties frequently refer to themselves Christian Democrat—the PAN in Mexico, for example.

The Aprista Parties. In perhaps half of the republics there exi parties of the moderate democratic Left that one could group loose as *aprista,* after the oldest and most prominent of the group, t APRA (*Alianza Popular Revolucionaria Americana*) of Peru. Lik the Christian Democrats, these are parties of recent origin; unli all the parties listed heretofore, they fall outside the categories the traditional European party systems. Accordingly, some write have stressed their indigenous American character, although act ally parties comparable in program and sources of support have d veloped in recent years in Africa and Asia.

The impulse that animates the *aprista* parties might loosely termed "socialist" in the general sense in which the Christian Dem crats are referred to as Christian Socialists; indeed, *aprista* leade often refer to themselves as "socialist." They differ clearly from t Socialist parties proper, however, in being pragmatic, unbound doctrine, not committed to nationalization of economic enterpris on principle, certainly not Marxist. *Aprista* parties in power ha shown themselves flexible and realistic, for example, encouraging controlling private economic enterprise as the needs of the econom ned to indicate, being prepared to cooperate with the United tes if North American purposes seem worthy of support, and ching accommodations with the Church without either favoritism persecution. The voluminous writings of Haya de la Torre and counterparts in other countries notwithstanding, what has ded *aprista* leaders has been not doctrine but general principles sympathy with the underprivileged, the maintenance of political nocracy, and national progress and development. In these respects might compare parties of this type with the Democratic parties the Northern United States.[13]

The social bases of the parties' support are principally to be found ong organized labor; the organized peasantry; and intellectuals. e major parties that could probably be denominated as *aprista* outlook and program are, of course, the APRA itself, in Peru; *ión Democrática* in Venezuela; the *Febreristas* in Paraguay; the *tido Revolucionario* of President Mendéz Montenegro, in Guatela; the *Partido Revolucionario Dominicano* in the Dominican public; the *Liberación Nacional* in Costa Rica; and possibly also *Movimiento Nacional Revolucionario* in Bolivia and the Mexa *Partido Revolucionario Institucional,* although the special cirnstances in which the latter two parties came to power endow m with certain distinctive characteristics that will be discussed r. In addition, there are *aprista* elements within the area's Liberal l Radical parties.

t is interesting to note that, except for the *Febreristas,* the *aprista* ties cited above are all either in power at present or have held ver in recent years. Once in power, frequently the parties' pragtism and sense for realities have led to policies too moderate for younger and more extreme members, who then secede to the t. This has happened most notably to *Acción Democrática* in nezuela, and also to the APRA itself, which has not been in power has supported a moderate conservative government; the radical- of the younger members of PRD was an important factor in

Or perhaps more exactly with the ADA (Americans for Democratic Ac-).

shaping the course of events that led to United States interventi in the Dominican Republic during 1965.

Just as there are Communist and Socialist "Internationals," *apri* parties hold international meetings and maintain contact with ea other, although in a less formal way. In addition, José Figueres, President of Costa Rica and founder of the *Partido Liberaci Nacional,* has started the Institute for Political Education, whi offers a short course in economics, international relations, and pr tical political action for young future leaders of the parties of democratic Left. The PLN also used to publish a political journ *Combate,* which was well-known in the hemisphere.

Socialist Parties. Socialist parties have been, on the whole, of most as little political significance in Latin America as they ha in the United States. With the exception of Chile, Socialist part have never been able to entertain any realistic hope of coming power by winning elections. Perhaps before one discusses the pr pects of the Socialist parties in the Latin American republics, ho ever, one should first make some fundamental distinctions abo parties called "socialist," since the word has come to have varyi meanings and certainly varying connotations.

The traditional Socialist parties of Latin America strongly semble European Socialist parties, and indeed have flourished es cially in the states of southern South America to which Europe immigrants came in great numbers during the second half of nineteenth century, the major period of growth of the Socia movement. These parties have been on the whole doctrinaire ponents of the capitalist system on principle, regardless of its p formance as a producer of goods and services, and have been conte with doctrinal purity and a small intellectual following, plus so working-class supporters. Their programs were not adapted to co temporary issues, but stressed instead a fundamental view of a sirable form of economy and society; issues of international relatio were secondary by a long way. Perhaps Senator Alfredo Palacios Argentina represents this classic type of Socialist at its grandestan high in public esteem, respected for his integrity, but without chance of entering a government: not unlike Norman Thomas the United States, although better known and rather more sucssful electorally!

Because of the fragmented nature of the party systems in Ecuador d Chile, individual Socialist party members have been Cabinet inisters in those countries under several Presidents, despite the nited following of the parties themselves. In addition, a handful Socialist party representatives can be found in the national legisures of Argentina, Brazil, and Uruguay.

Parties of a quite different type have recently been appearing, metimes under the name "Popular Socialist." These parties, alough they call for domestic social reform, are especially concerned th the international scene. They more often follow the lead of ommunist China than that of the Soviet Union, but most often lay ecial stress on their sympathies with the government of Fidel Cas- in Cuba. In domestic politics, they stand ready to cooperate with cal Communist parties—indeed they enroll individual Communists members—and they are prepared to countenance violence to hieve their objectives, if necessary. In this last respect they often do t differ markedly from some of the other Latin American parties, course, but the contrast with the traditional Socialist parties is ite marked. A list of current "Popular Socialist" parties, or protorties, would have to include the Fourteenth of June Movement the Dominican Republic, the movement headed by Francisco lião in Brazil (the Peasant Leagues of Resistance), the *Partido volucionario Abril y Mayo* in El Salvador, the *Partido de Unidad volucionaria* in Guatemala, the *Movimiento de Izquierda Revolunaria* in Venezuela and Peru, Fidel Castro's own Communist rty of Cuba, and groups elsewhere called *Frentes* (or *Moviientos*) *de Liberación Nacional.* In addition, there are Popular cialist elements within several other Latin American parties and litical movements, whose unhappy leaders have to try to prevent eir organizations from disintegrating in the split between *Fidelista* and more moderate elements. Dissident wings have already, at th time of writing, split off from *aprista* parties and formed ne groups over this and related issues; the *Movimiento de Izquierd Revolucionaria* (MIR) was formed from the youth movement *Acción Democrática* in Venezuela, for example.

Popular Socialist parties are strongest among students, the ci poor, and in some cases the peasants, although there is general also some support from dissident union members. These are parti that do not seem likely today to come to power through the ballo but in a revolutionary situation might be in a position to sei power, a possibility for which some of them prepare actively.

The only governing party of this type is found in Cuba. The it has put into effect a program resembling that of the Soviet Com munist party—only more so. That is, it has gone farther faster tha the Soviet Communist Party: in moving more swiftly into the "sta farm" organization of agriculture, without a long "collective farm stage (in Soviet theory, the state farm is regarded as a more a vanced form of organization than the collective farm, which st retains individualistic elements); in renouncing elections, instead at least going through the forms of an election process, as is do in the Soviet Union; in instituting statist forms of economic orga ization on a schedule of maximum acceleration, so far at least wit out the concessions to individualism (for example, the New Ec nomic Policy, the relaxation after Stalin's "Dizzy with Succes speech, or Premier Khrushchev's decentralization program) th have marked the process within the Soviet Union.

A realistic appraisal of the Popular Socialist parties might w lead to the view that they are more "Left" than the Communist that they represent, in fact, a kind of neo-Trotskyite position. Th can be said because the Communist parties themselves, since th organization in their present form after the Bolshevik Revolutio have placed loyalty to the Soviet Union, as the "first Socialist stat and the leader of the world proletarian movement, ahead of oth considerations. This primary loyalty to the Soviet Union has mea that the party line at any one time soft-pedals or abandons temp arily its long-term economic and political goals. Thus, during the period of the Popular Front in the 1930s, the main danger to the Soviet Union was that of aggressive Nazism and fascism, and other objectives were subordinated to the struggle against fascism. Accordingly, local Communist parties temporarily dropped attacks on the democratic parties, and rallied behind democratic leaders who opposed fascism in the international arena. Extreme revolutionary parties which, while cooperating on occasion with the international Communist movement, do not form part of it, are under no such compulsion to forgo their own domestic programs in the interest of the requirements of Soviet foreign policy. They can thus pursue a doggedly violent and revolutionary line with consistency, ignoring the twists and turns of Soviet policy to which loyal Communists must pay so much attention. An attitude of this kind is regarded by the Communists as "Left-wing dogmatism" and even Trotskyism, Trotsky himself having advocated the pursuit of a consistent "hard" policy of violent revolution.

It is clear therefore that in some ways a Popular Socialist movement may constitute a greater danger to the established constitutional order in any given country than the local Communist party itself, disciplined, dedicated, and supported by the Soviet Union though it may be. This is so because the allegiance to the Soviet Union that is the first principle of the local Communist party leads it to make sudden shifts of position in response to changes in Soviet policies that make its dependence on foreign guidance clear, and make it appear disloyal and even rather ridiculous. Moreover, the local party leaders are usually older men comfortably settled in bureaucratic jobs as union leaders or editors of the party newspaper, who would be nonplussed or frightened at the prospect of actually leading a revolution. At the same time, the party often loses popular support because its Soviet-inspired tactical line is not suitable to local conditions. An autonomous Popular Socialist movement does not carry liabilities of this type, and younger revolutionaries are often contemptuous of the "conservative" leadership and policies of the established Communist parties.

One of the distinctions between the "traditional" Socialist party and the new "Popular Socialist" movements is that the traditional Socialists were normally reluctant to cooperate with the Communists, and often were strongly anti-Communist, the Communists representing a perverted variety of socialism and being their rivals for working-class support; whereas the Popular Socialists, as we have seen, are pro-Communist and willing to cooperate with the local Communist party. A major exception to this general rule, however, can be found in Chile. There, almost continuously since 1936 the traditional Socialist party has been in coalition with the Communist party and some smaller left-wing groups in a "Popular Front" for electoral purposes.[14] The Chilean Socialist party is proportionately the strongest in the hemisphere, if one excepts the governing party of Cuba, and it shares control of the labor movement with the Communists. In this, as in other respects, Chilean and French politics strongly resemble each other.

Communist Parties. Latin American Communists loom larger in the consciousness of North Americans or of Right-wing Latin Americans than they do in reality. This is due in part to imprecision in political discourse; in part to ignorance; in part to the tactics of the Communist movement since Lenin's day of insinuating its members into non-Communist organizations, which they try to dominate and in whose name they try to act; and in large part to the fact that since Communism is unpopular, unscrupulous politicians habitually call their liberal and Left-wing opponents "Communists" in order to discredit them. This is a favorite technique of dictators, of course of such ancient standing and used by men who lie so continually that North Americans by now should really know enough to look beyond the name-calling to the facts—should, but often don't. In some cases, the instinctive reaction of the dictator and the Right wing demagogue to call his democratic opponents "Communists" reaches really ludicrous extremes, as when the present President of

[14] The Radical party, which provided the Popular Front's Presidential candidates during most of its first ten years of existence—two of them successful—is no longer part of the grouping.

Haiti, François Duvalier, in November of 1960 actually expelled the Archbishop of Port-au-Prince, François Poirier, on charges of financing Communist activities.

One of the problems in trying to gauge correctly the extent of Communist strength in Latin America is that in almost all the republics the party is outlawed, either specifically by name, or under the terms of a general statute prohibiting parties that advocate violent revolution or that are controlled from abroad. Currently, the party is fully legal only in Chile, Uruguay, the Dominican Republic and Cuba. Where it is outlawed, it continues to operate as a political party anyhow if it can, either on its own under another name, or else within a "Popular Socialist" or "Labor" party. Even where it may operate legally, however, the party maintains a clandestine organization against the day when it may have to go underground.

Although the Right-wing dictator always makes a conspicuous display of his anti-Communism (especially if he is seeking economic aid from the United States), the Communists have actually been able to work out mutually satisfactory arrangements with ostensibly anti-Communist dictators; for example, in return for a free hand in infiltrating labor union leadership, they can offer freedom from "labor trouble" to the dictator. Among recent dictators, Fulgencio Batista is reputed to have had an arrangement of this kind with the Cuban Communists, even though the party was legally dissolved. Perón and Vargas, Ibáñez and Odría, have also found it possible to cooperate with local Communists on occasion. When the Communists undertake this type of arrangement with a dictator, however, the standard procedure is to take out insurance by maintaining contact with the opposition, in exile or underground. What has happened in such cases is that the party has ostensibly "split," one wing supporting, the other opposing, the regime, so that the party is well-connected whether the regime continues or is overthrown.

Where it meets with a regime receptive to its overtures, of course, the party endeavors to have loyal members appointed to official positions, with the hope that some day it will be in a position to dominate the government. This policy was temporarily successful in Guatemala under the Presidency of Jacobo Arbenz Guzmán (1951-54), and has been a smashing success so far in Cuba under the regime led by Fidel Castro Ruz. By affording Fidel Castro a hard-working, conscientious cadre of men willing to give concrete effect to his vague revolutionary aspirations, and by "educating" Castro himself into seeing that his nebulous Leftist ideas could be made sense of in a Marxist framework, Communists were accepted into the Revolutionary government of Cuba, although Fidel Castro has always made it clear that he, not the party, is in control.

Today the party's strength, outside Cuba, is probably greatest in Chile, Brazil, and Venezuela. It is a minor political factor in Uruguay and Argentina, and has at least some intellectual influence in Peru, Mexico, Guatemala, and Panama. Elsewhere the party is without significance, so far as one can see at the present time. In Chile it is strongest among organized labor, in Venezuela among the city poor, in Brazil among the city poor at present and probably among the peasantry of the depressed Northeast states in the future.

Personalist and Caudillo *Parties.* In Latin American political life, heavy stress is placed upon individual political leaders. Parties and political tendencies within parties are often known by the names of their leaders, even after these leaders have passed on. Sometimes the party bears the leader's name not as an informal soubriquet, but as the formal party title—for example, Perón's party was officially the *Partido Peronista,* that of Velasco Ibarra of Ecuador the *Federación Nacional Velasquista.*

To be sure, this phenomenon is not unknown outside of Latin America. The name of a well-known political figure often serves as a shorthand description of a political tendency in the United States, for example; one speaks of Taft or of Goldwater Republicans. However, there is a considerable difference between the designation of a party or political tendency by the name of an individual where this is used for purposes of identification and easy reference, and where its significance is that the party exists to put the leader in power nd has no autonomous existence nor a specific program other than endorse his views.

Political organizations of the latter type may be called personalist arties. They abound in Latin America (and in other areas that are t comparable stages of political development) especially, as we have lready noted, because of the limited development of the political ystems of the states of the area. Loyalties to persons fill the void ft by the absence of continuing representative institutions or organizations that should command loyalty. Panama or, more strikngly, Haiti, provide classic examples of personalism of this type. n addition, loyalty to a commanding personality provides a cement olding together individuals for purposes of common political action here because of the rudimentary development of the country's social technology," the organizational mechanisms that perform nis function elsewhere are absent. In the unordered chaos of the ountry's political life, dominant individuals provide the only rallyng points. In Haiti, personalist domination of politics is complete; invades the political systems elsewhere to varying extents, so that nere may be one or two permanently organized, doctrinally sophiscated, modern political parties, competing with an array of personist groupings. Indeed, it may be that any given political party is self compounded of personalist and non-personalist factors in unasy coexistence.

Personalism is especially a feature of the political life of the less dvanced, less organized, smaller, poorer countries. When it emerges nd develops to significant proportions in advanced societies, it can e taken as evidence of crisis and the breakdown of normal and able political patterns, as the cases of the personalist attractiveness f Roosevelt in the United States, Churchill in Britain, and De Gaulle in France demonstrate. (One might almost say "Blessed the country without great men; for its troubles are small.")

In the republics where effective political participation is confined a small social class, the personalist party may be no more than small clique gathered around some prominent political figure;

this is predominantly the case in Panama, for example. Alternatively the personalist party may support the type of figure Rosendo A Gomez has called the demagogic *caudillo,* the authoritarian persona leader who rules, or aspires to rule, not simply by force and fea but with the aid of a mass popular following.

One can consider the "*caudillo* party" as a special category c party in an ideological spectrum because, by virtue of its personalism and its mobilization of mass support, a party of this kind *necessaril* has a distinctive type of ideology, or pseudo-ideology.

In recent years, the leading examples of the *caudillo* party hav been the *Partido Peronista* in Argentina, the *Unión Naciona Odriísta* in Peru, the *Federación Nacional Velasquista* in Ecuado Rojas Pinilla's *Alianza Nacional Popular* (ANAPO) in Colombi Ibáñez del Campo's Farmer-Labor party in Chile, and the Nationa Republican Party of Rafael Angel Calderón Guardia in Costa Ric Generals Odría of Peru, Ibáñez of Chile, and Rojas Pinilla c Colombia, all of whom originally came to power by means of th military *coup,* only emerged as real demagogues after their de partures from the President's chair, each trying to build up a popula following in the attempt to stage a comeback. One way to di tinguish the classic military or paternalistic dictator from the dema gogic *caudillo* is that the latter, once deposed, has the popular follow ing to make an attempt at a comeback in a democratic election wit a reasonable chance of success. Both Velasco and Ibáñez, cited abov succeeded in this feat, as did Getúlio Vargas of Brazil (of whon more later). Rojas, Odría, and Calderón have made the attemp while Perón is deterred from it only by legal rulings against h candidacy.

The principal features of the "*caudillo* party's" ideology are th following. In the first place, since it aims to concentrate power i the hands of one man, it stresses the need for leadership and decri the slowness, the cumbersomeness, and the alleged injustice of co stitutional forms. Then, since it attempts to build a mass followin the party necessarily promises—in however cloudy terms—soci progress, improvement in the lot of the masses, and the upliftin the downtrodden. Yet since the party is founded on the sheer sire to achieve power and build a following, the party's ideology d stated goals are simply the most appropriate weapons in the ruggle; they are thus *ad hoc,* nebulous, lacking in content, and be modified or abandoned if tactical requirements so indicate. he party is prepared to use violence, especially once in power— nce the achievement and retention of power is the movement's ime *raison d'être*. Nor is it reluctant to preach a gospel of hate d aggression—against the well-to-do, the foreigner, and the move- ent's opponents. In sum, the ideology of the "*caudillo* party" is thoritarian, pseudo-socialist, nationalist, aggressive, eclectic.

The party thus presents many faces to the observer, and is likely elude being placed in the traditional series of categories. Consider, r example, how some of the most able observers of the Latin merican scene have characterized the movement led by Juan rón. Robert J. Alexander has most recently classed Perón with e "Jacobin Left," which also includes Fidel Castro; and indeed in e demagoguery, the anti-Yankeeism, the championing of the dis- ssessed, there are clear resemblances between the Argentine and e Cuban. William W. Pierson and Federico G. Gil categorize ronism, as an indigenous, nationalist, labor-oriented movement, ith the *aprista* parties; and one can find similarities between the o, with the National Revolutionary movement in Bolivia serving a sort of "missing link," especially in its early years, when it was rectly influenced by Peronism, and was more prone to violence, d a great deal more anti-Yankee, than it has since become.

It used to go without saying that Perón was a fascist; and perhaps is is still the best category, in the lexicon of European politics, in hich to place him. Clearly, Perón studied Mussolini's techniques first hand while a military attaché in Italy; his demagoguery and e of force were quite fascist-like (again using "fascist" in its Italian notation); and, like Mussolini, he raised insincerity and op- rtunism to a high principle—Perón said of his *Justicialismo* what ussolini had written of fascism, that its essence was to be prag- atic, to meet each problem on its own terms, not with some predetermined set of solutions. Harold E. Davis has aptly compare Peronism with "other modern fascist-like regimes which have trie to clothe their naked quest for power with the respectable garment of an ideology."[15] Like Franco, to carry the parallel further, Peró was also fond of describing his position as a third one, "between the mistaken poles of Communism and capitalism, thus making i appear moderate and reasonable. However, if there is one clea characteristic of the "*caudillo* party" and its leader, it is that the can always attract and work with extremists—national chauvinist Communists, authoritarians: with all men of violence and hatred— never with liberals, moderates, democrats, constitutionalists.

There is a story that a Minister of the Interior told Curnonsk the noted French epicure, that before approving him for the awar of the Legion of Honor, he had checked his police dossier for "politi cal reliability," and found not one, but two sets of records. Unde "Curnonsky," which was a nom-de-plume, he found an account c the doings of an anarchist and Bolshevik of disorderly habits an disreputable associates; under the gourmet's real name were liste the activities of a reactionary and active Royalist, who regularl dined with the Count of Paris, the pretender to the throne. "Well, the minister told him, "I averaged the two and decided you were loyal republican." The same effect is often visible in appraisals of th *caudillo* party; the observer averages its Right and Left supporter the reactionaries and the radicals, the military authoritarians an the haranguers of street crowds, and concludes that it must be "center" grouping. This has been the burden of much of the dis cussion of the followers of Ibáñez in Chile, of Velasco Ibarra i Ecuador, of Calderón Guardia in Costa Rica, for example, all c whom have been supported at one time or another by both con servative nationalists and Communists. The demagogic *caudillo* at tracts supporters from both extremes of the spectrum because, al though he speaks to the mobs in the words they wish to hear, con

[15] Harold E. Davis, ed., *Government and Politics in Latin America* (Ronal New York, 1958), p. 112.

rvative authoritarians can hope that he will provide the "strong ınd" that will discipline the people to obedience.[16]

When in power the *caudillo's* policies may even continue to satisfy ›th elements, though commonly those at one extreme (the dynam- ; of governing being what they are, it is usually the Left) complain ›out the leader's having been captured, or having sold out.

This ambiguity in the demagogic *caudillo's* attractive power to ese two forces—authority and poverty—comes through quite :arly in the case of Getúlio Vargas of Brazil, although Vargas did ithout the harshness and needless cruelty that characterize the ctators of the Hispanic countries, and was supported by moderates well as extremists. Vargas was able to rule the country well ›ough without an organized party, on a personal basis; parties ıve been relatively unimportant in Brazilian politics, in any case. 'hen Vargas, who was always the height of flexibility, decided at e end of World War II that democracy was back in fashion, and epared to get himself confirmed in the Presidency by election, he ganized a political party, the Social Democrats, out of his ad- inistrative appointees in the state governments; this is now a con- rvative party, if one can give Brazilian parties ideological labels. ıortly thereafter, the dictator was deposed by a military *coup,* and epared a comeback by organizing as an appropriate vehicle the razilian Labor Party, based on the labor movement, which had :nefited from legislation adopted during his term. Originally, argas had intended to organize officeholders and unionists into a ngle party, but had been dissuaded by an advisor on the basis that e two elements would be incompatible, and nothing would be lost ' creating two parties rather than one.

ıRTY SYSTEMS AND ELECTORAL SYSTEMS

We have looked so far at the internal determinants of a party's :havior—its ideology and the social forces it represents. But the ırty's actions are also shaped by the environment in which it must

[16] A similar pattern was visible in Hitler's following.

operate: the organization of the government that it seeks to contr of course, but also the nature of its competition—the other parties- and the rules that determine success or failure in the party battle- the electoral system. Since the party system and the electoral syste in each country are closely related, they will be discussed togethe Before getting into the detailed discussion, however, let us fir glance briefly at one of the leading theoretical questions in empiric political science, that of the causal relation between party syste and electoral system.

What determines whether a country will have a system in whic two major parties compete, or one in which a half-dozen "mediu sized" groups contend for power? [17] The answer that probably t majority of students of the problem would give is that the cruci determinant is the electoral system; if representatives are elected i "single-member districts," that is, where there is to be only one vict in the election, then the various groups will tend to coalesce in only two parties; otherwise, a multi-party system is to be expecte This is so, runs the argument, since in a single-member election t victor needs to garner at least 50% + 1 of the available vote Clearly, no more than two parties can have a reasonable expectatio of reaching this figure. Accordingly, third, fourth, and so on partie realizing the hopelessness of their cause, will join with the maj party they consider the lesser evil and try to realize their goals fro within it. Where representatives are elected in multi-member di tricts, however, the chances of the lesser parties are not hopeless all; they may elect a few representatives whose legislative votes w be valuable for bargaining purposes, and may even hope to hold balance of power. For example: under perfect proportional repr sentation (or as perfect as it can be without dividing legislators in fractions!) over the whole country—say, the current Israeli elector system—then a party garnering 7 per cent of the vote will take ju 7 per cent of the seats in the legislative assembly. That 7 per ce

[17] Here and throughout, the number of parties considered to be active in t party system will include only those groups that can entertain serious expect tions of being able to gain power and not the miniscule groups, to be four everywhere, which are taken seriously by no one but themselves.

ay be crucial in making up a government majority, and the party n expect to be able to exact a price, in concessions on policy ques- ›ns, and in office for party leaders, in return for its support. In ectoral systems based upon proportional representation principles, cordingly, there is no reason for the smaller parties to go out of ısiness and merge with a larger group—in fact there is every reason ›t to.

Various objections can be raised to this thesis. It presupposes, of ›urse, that party leaders and voters act rationally and will not ›ntinue to "waste" their efforts in a hopeless cause. Although this on the whole a sound assumption, exceptions to it certainly exist. [ore interesting is the object raised, among others, by Leslie ipson, that the electoral system does not after all create itself, but set up by a party or coalition of parties—normally in the expecta- ›n that its provisions will redound to the benefit of the groups that amed it. In other words, the party system may well antedate the ectoral system, and may determine *it,* rather than the other way ›ound. This in fact is probably what has happened in most coun- ies. It is, however, solely of historical interest and in no way iminates the causal relation between electoral system and party stem that was just described, but on the contrary assumes it; if ıe parties are interested in modifying the electoral laws in their terest, then clearly those laws must bear a significant causal rela- ›n to the party situation that will come to exist under them.

The best single case study in the causal relation between electoral stem and party system is surely provided by a glance at the situa- ›n in Brazil. In Brazilian legislative elections (under normal demo- atic conditions) rules of perfect proportionality apply; in addi- ›n, the voter votes not for the party as such, but for an individual ındidate on the party's list. The result is not only a multiplication parties (three major, two or three minor, and innumerable splin- r parties exist) but a kind of war of all against all, since even ındidates on the same party list are, to some extent, competing ith each other for votes. This is the multi-party system carried to -and past—its logical conclusion. Yet in elections to fill single

offices in Brazil, those of President, Vice-President, Governor, an
Senator, the dynamics of the two-party system are clearly at worl
Out of a welter of furious inter-group bargaining before each ele
tion emerge, in the typical case, two major coalition slates of cand
dates for the single offices to be filled; minor and splinter party thir
candidacies occur, especially as a consequence of stalemate an
breakdown of the ticket-writing negotiations, but they are clear
hopeless gestures, about on the vote-drawing level of third-part
candidacies in U. S. Presidential elections. This contrast betwee
legislative and Presidential or Gubernatorial elections in Brazil pr
vides a graphic illustration of the validity of the imputed caus
relationship between the single-office election and the two-part
system.[18]

The Multi-Party System. The multi-party system is the mo
widespread in Latin America, occurring in over half of the repu
lics, although in different forms. The stability of the parties in suc
a system can vary over a wide range, from the situation in Chi
where the major parties, with one exception, are all over 50 yea
old, to that in Panama, El Salvador, or Haiti, where most parti
do not date back more than two Presidential elections.

The relative importance in determining the voter's choice of th
party itself, the party leader, and the individual candidate, also vari
widely. As was noted, the influence of the personality of the part
leader is greatest in the smaller and more backward republics. Bu
the electoral laws are important here, too. It was mentioned pr
viously, for example, that in Brazil the voter indicates his preferen
for the individual candidate, rather than for the party. Votes th
the candidate receives over and above the quota necessary to ele
him are credited to the other candidates on the party ticket. Pa
ticularly strong candidates are accordingly in a position to bargai
with different parties for the best arrangement they can obtain, i
terms of running-mates, the party's position on policy questions, et

[18] In Chile, victorious Presidential candidates normally represent coalitio
also, but inter-party hostility is stronger than in Brazil, and coalition negoti
tions break down more frequently.

Jnder the Brazilian system, it was even possible for Jânio Quadros, political independent, a man without party affiliation, to go all he way to the Presidency. In Chile, on the other hand, balloting rrangements make it easier for the voter to have a choice of voting ither for an individual candidate or for the party list as a whole, which gives the party its own votes, as it were, making it less posible for an individual candidate to bargain with the party on terms f equality. Within the category of multi-party systems, then, there xists a wide latitude for variation in the degree of personalism, which will reflect provisions of the electoral laws as well as factors n the political culture of the country concerned. There is, however, well-established syndrome of characteristics typical of the multiarty system as such.

In the first place, there is the tendency for the number of parties o proliferate indefinitely. If the nation's electoral laws allow small olitical groupings to secure legislative representation, there is obiously no inducement to channel political activity through an aleady existing party rather than create another one. To contain the arty system within intelligible bounds, therefore, the standard pracice is for the electoral laws to prescribe minimum conditions that arties must fulfill to be registered with the electoral tribunals and ffer candidates. Apart from technical requirements, such as the eporting of the names of party officials, the key requirement is norally that a new party demonstrate a certain minimum of support efore it can be registered; usually it must submit petitions containng a specified number of signatures. Although provisions of this ype may act to exclude the most minuscule of splinter groups, a letermined new party can usually find enough people to sign its etitions. Registration requirements, on the other hand, are liable o abuse, which occurs frequently, in being used by partisan officials o disqualify opposition parties and candidates on the basis of some ninor technical infringement.

A more basic difficulty of the multi-party system is that, since the arties labor under no compulsion to try to put together a winning oalition of 50% + 1 of the voters for the legislative elections, they can afford the luxury of extreme and demagogic appeals tha might alienate moderates but will win votes elsewhere. That is, i a multi-party system, it makes most sense for a party to fix on on or two substantial opinion-and-interest groups in the electorate, an try to capture their allegiance by outbidding the other parties fo their support. The emphasis is not on moderation and inclusivenes as in the classic model of the two-party system, but on extremisn and one-sidedness, conducive to the deepening of political cleavage and a greater readiness to resort to violence.

This is a particularly explosive mixture in the multi-party systen because in the nature of things no one party will be able to gain clear-cut electoral victory. The parties which, during the electior vied with each other in mutual vituperation, now find that th passage of legislation requires that they cooperate in forming parliamentary majority. If such a majority can come into being– and it may not, creating a legislative stalemate and an invitation t Presidential dictatorship—it will be weak, internally divided, agree only on a minimal program, and likely at any time to split an plunge the law-making processes into disorder. If the parties d manage to cooperate, on the other hand, even for a limited perioc after an election campaign of mutual enmity and recrimination, thi can only seem to the voter like the crudest kind of expediency whic sacrifices principle to political ambition. The system has thus built-in cynicism-producing effect.

Presidential elections in a multi-party system, subject to th dynamic processes of uninomial (single-office) elections, have th effect of inducing pre-election party coalitions, as was noted above In Brazil and Chile, for example, attempts at forming coalitions fo the Presidential elections are always made. In the two Presidentia elections since 1954 in which the vote was free, the two par ties founded by Vargas, the Social Democrats (PSD) and th Brazilian Labor Party (PTB), have run a coalition candidate agains the anti-Vargas UDN (National Democratic Union). In Chilea Presidential elections since the 1930s, the parties of the Left hav coalesced on a single candidate, a Radical where the Radical Part as joined the coalition, a Socialist where it has not; while the Jnited Conservatives and the Liberals have likewise taken to running a joint candidate. In the 1958 and 1964 elections, these two oalition candidates were joined by one from the Christian Demoratic party, which felt itself unable to join either coalition, and a epresentative of the Radicals, who could join with either but were ndecided as to which.

Coalitions of a different type—"silent coalitions," one might say—ave recently occurred in Presidential elections in Peru, Venezuela, nd Argentina. During the periods of APRA's illegality in Peru, ie party used unofficially to endorse the candidates of other parties; *lcción Democrática* acted similarly during the Pérez Jiménez dictorship in Venezuela; while in the 1958 Argentine Presidential lection, exiled dictator Juan Perón urged supporters of his outlawed arty to cast their votes for Arturo Frondizi, the candidate of the ntransigent Radicals.

Quite frequently, however, the successful Presidential candidate ı multi-party elections represents a minority of the voters. The arties are too used to opposing each other in legislative elections) be able to coalesce on common Presidential candidacies. This ecessarily means that the President will encounter great difficulties, ı the legislature and in the country, in giving effect to his program.

Finally, the frequent mutations in the number of parties operating nd in the coalitions formed, together with the ease with which a ersonalist leader can attract a following, mean that the system is ı a constant state of flux, that quite different governing configuraons emerge, and that policy lacks stability and continuity.

The Two-Party System. There are still what might be called twoarty systems in several Latin American states: Colombia, Uruguay, Ionduras, and Nicaragua, although in most of the republics the stablished two-party systems that were inherited from the nineeenth century were not able to contain the range of issues that beame active during the twentieth century. The two-party system as preserved itself in each case for a variety of specific reasons, vhich may include: a favorable set of electoral laws (for example, the single-member district for legislative elections); the fact that the Liberal leaders proved flexible and open to new ideas; and a fierce inherited party loyalty stemming from memories of bitter civil war between the two parties.

Even where the two-party system continues in form, however, the range of political opinion has proved too broad to be expressed by only two alternatives, and the presence of more or less permanent factions within the two major parties is the standard situation. Permanent factionalism is especially characteristic of the two-party system, in point of fact; where party identification expresses an inherited loyalty, it is unavailable as an expression of opinion—to express a novel point of view, one creates a new faction rather than a new party.

Permanent factionalism is recognized by the Uruguayan electoral system, with provision being made for the combination of the votes cast for the factions within each party in the elections to the National Council, the country's collegial executive. In effect, the electoral law provides for a kind of simultaneous primary and general election, with victory going to the candidates of the majority faction of the majority party (who might have fewer votes than the candidates of the major faction of the minority party).

Permanently existing factions characterize the Colombian two-party system, also, the Conservatives being divided currently into Laureanistas and Ospinistas, after the names of the factional leaders, the Liberals being split between "doctrinaires," who form a substantial majority of the party, and the followers of Adolfo López Michelsen, who are organized as the Liberal Revolutionary Movement, or MRL.

In Nicaragua, also, the Liberal party has split as a result of its conversion into an organ of the dictatorship of the late Anastasio Somoza, currently being continued by his sons. The official party is the *Partido Liberal Nacional,* the anti-Somoza exile group taking the name *Partido Liberal Independiente.* The Conservatives have split along similar lines.

In Honduras the Nationalists (Conservatives) split between suprters and opponents of dictator Carías Andino; however, the two oups often cooperate and run joint candidates.

Thus, even in the normally two-party system, the groups actuy competing for power may be more than one might guess on perficial acquaintance. On the other hand, a device has been deloped for moderating the scope of the power struggle among the rties. This is guaranteed minority representation, which has placed strict proportionality as the constitutive principle of some the Latin American legislatures. Thus in Argentina, under the -called Sáenz Peña law of 1912, which was revived after the overrow of Perón but was subsequently replaced by a proporonal representation system, minority parties are guaranteed at least e-third of the seats in the Chamber of Deputies by the provision at the voter can mark his ballot for candidates for only two-thirds the vacancies. There used to be minority representation provisions Cuban electoral legislation, also.

In Uruguay the principle of guaranteed minority representation currently given effect in the republic's nine-man collegial execuve, on which the seats are distributed in the ratio of six to three tween the majority and the minority parties.

Colombia, as a result of the tragic experiences of over a decade bitter guerrilla warfare between Conservative and Liberal partins, together with the experience of cooperation between leaders of e two parties in the overthrow and liquidation of the dictatorship General Rojas Pinilla, has gone a step further in this direction d established parity of representation for the two parties in all gislative organs and in the President's cabinet. This statesmanlike novation, the National Front agreement, also stipulated that the vo parties would alternate in the Presidency for a period of 12 ars.[19] It was drawn up by party leaders Laureano Gómez for the onservatives and Alberto Lleras Camargo for the Liberals in the act of Sitges of July, 1957, when both were in exile from the Rojas inilla dictatorship. Although the agreement was embodied in an nendment to the Constitution after the dictatorship was over-

[19] Subsequently extended to 16 years.

thrown, it is currently under attack from both ends of the politic spectrum (having been repudiated by Laureano), although at pre ent the weight of the country's opinion seems to continue in i favor, as was evidenced by the substantial margin of support give the National Front candidate in the 1966 Presidential elections.

The One-Party System. Perhaps most people would automaticall identify a political system in which there was only one major part in which everybody knew in advance that the government's Pres dential candidate would be victorious, as a dictatorship. And ce tainly, most dictatorships do in fact establish an official party, whic monopolizes electoral office, prohibiting or barely tolerating oppo sition groups. Present-day Cuba clearly falls into the category of th single-party dictatorship, for example.

On the other hand, there is in Mexico an example of a one-part system that tolerates the existence of opposition parties and cand dates for office, and allows the full range of civil liberties one ass ciates with a free and democratic state. (Bolivia had until 1964 a one party system, also somewhat less democratic than Mexico's. Today this does not seem quite as strange as it did a decade ag since we have become familiar with the democratic one-party syster in so many of the newly independent states of Africa and Asi (some of which have *non*-democratic one-party systems, also, to b sure).

At first sight, it certainly seems a paradox that a majority part which permits an opposition to develop can retain a monopol on political power. Why are not all democracies two- or multi-part systems? Of course, in the long run, they are. Dissatisfaction wit the incumbent party steadily increases until the opposition find itself able to make a successful bid for power. But the long run ca take a very long time to become reality. Thus, the conservative op position party in Mexico, the Party of National Action (PAN), ha steadily increased its vote in legislative elections since its foundin over 20 years ago, but the rate of increase is slow enough that if i continues at the same amplitude, at the very least another 20 year will pass before the PAN can be within striking distance of a legisl e majority. In other words, one-party politics represents a depar- e from an equilibrium two- or multi-party system, and some day : equilibrium position will be reached; but that day may be off. Meanwhile, a democratic one-party system exists.

The PRI in Mexico bears some resemblance to the African gle parties in being based on a revolutionary nationalist *mystique,* d on the enthusiasm that nationalist revolution engenders. In Mex- the importance of the charismatic leader no longer approaches : African norm, however, while the PRI is based on coalition of nomic interest groups, with potentially conflicting interests, not a population of fairly homogeneous economic character.

This necessity to reconcile the interests of a variety of economic ups under which the leadership of the official party in Mexico ors impose the necessity of performing miracles of conjuring and lancing in order to maintain the solidarity of the revolutionary rty. This has been facilitated, and perhaps made possible, in exico by the existence of a steadily expanding economy, so that : claims of the various groups could be at least progressively satis- d without inhibiting the satisfaction of the claims of rival groups. ie Bolivian leadership was faced, on the other hand, with the all- t-impossible task of trying to pacify several key economic groups ile the economy was actually shrinking; clearly, this kind of thing s possible only in the short run, and the overthrow of the MNR gime took place in 1964 partly as a reaction to the repressive licies prompted by the opposition of disaffected groups.

It is thus of first importance, in the years immediately following : Revolution, that these economic groups continue to maintain eir uneasy alliance, for if they do not, armed conflict remains an er-present possibility. Mexico has now passed that stage; Bolivia ll has not done so.

One could in fact regard the function of the one-party system as at of maintaining a balance among divergent interests long ough so that the habit of settling disputes by violence is lost. In is the Mexican party has in all probability succeeded, overcoming historical tradition of constant civil war and political violence.

This is also the function that the Colombian National Front is d
signed to perform, using rather comparable techniques, although nc
the single-party mechanism.

The democratic one-party system can thus be viewed as a devic
appropriate to a stage of transition between the unity of a victoriou
revolutionary movement and the divisions of party politics norm
to a democracy. Its value lies in allowing the turbulence of the revo
lutionary period to subside, in fostering patterns of peaceful politic
and in allowing the expression of views and the organization fc
political purposes normal to a democracy, while foreclosing the po
sibility that this will lead to violence and renewed civil war. How
ever, it is solely valuable as making the transition possible, and if
succeeds it will eventually restore the country to multi-party politic
That is, in succeeding, the one-party system liquidates itself.

[Government Processes

A. CONSTITUTIONS

: GENERAL CONTENT OF CONSTITUTIONS

;onstitutions always specify the organization of public powers; t is, they establish the various organs of government and define relations among them. In addition, they set limits to the power lded by the governmental structure as a whole—they define in-idual rights. Quite frequently, and especially today, constitutions icate, often in considerable detail, the purposes government is igned to serve. In the recent constitutions, this latter function is ied to the point that the constitutional document contains what 1 effect a general outline of the policies government should fol-

.

1 their delineation of general governmental structure, the con-itions of the Latin American republics generally follow the stitution of the United States. Uniformly, they adopt the separa-of powers, rather than the concentration of powers in the legis-ve body characteristic of parliamentary systems. Almost invari-, they provide for strong presidencies, although Uruguay has ex-mented with a collegial executive council, and other countries e occasionally made provision for a Prime Minister dependent on gislative majority.[1] In addition, Mexico, Argentina, and Brazil e federal systems based on the North American model.

\t the time of writing, the Cuban constitution (of 1940) is in abeyance, the Prime Minister, Fidel Castro, wields dictatorial powers, ostensibly in :iation with a "collective leadership" of members of his cabinet and others. ezuela has a federal system in name only.

In the provisions governing individual rights, the courts, the a
ministrative system, and the internal organization of the legislatu
features of the Hispanic tradition are most in evidence, influenc
by French innovations of the Revolutionary and Napoleonic perio
In the sections on "social guarantees"—that is, those defining t
general aims of policy with respect to labor, social welfare, and t
economy in general—the strongest influence is probably that of t
Mexican Constitution of 1917, the first of the "modern" consti
tions in this respect.

THE FUNCTIONS OF THE LATIN AMERICAN CONSTITUTION

Quite clearly, many constitutional provisions are honored o
in the breach; and yet great stress is placed upon constitutio
forms and procedures, even where these mask political reali
quite discordant with their intent. National constitutions are heav
eulogized in popular oratory, and key provisions are well kno
and frequently cited; yet existing constitutions are frequently
carded and replaced—in fact the average life of Latin Ameri
constitutions has been slightly less than 20 years.

Nevertheless, a common pattern does exist despite these parado
One must distinguish, in the first place, between constitutio
provisions that prescribe the distribution of public powers, wh
organize governmental authority, and those that enjoin or im
specific government policies. The latter clauses, those embody
"social guarantees," stipulating that education is free and comp
sory, and so on, are not self-executing. They serve an exhortat
function, embodying national aspirations that should find express
in specific legislation and executive action where circumstan
make this feasible. Provisions of this kind set a direction for pul
policy, prescribing ultimate goals rather than providing imperat
mandates.

It is provisions of this kind that patriotic oratory regards as la
marks in the country's progress: the clause that establishes free p
lic education as a national principle, or announces that subsoil m

als belong to the whole nation. In these provisions, the nation has ken a stand, adopted a certain orientation, and made its policy sition clear.

The clauses that organize the public powers, prescribing the echanisms of constitutional succession and establishing the organs government, on the other hand, are literally followed in practice. may well be that the constitutional forms do not correspond to litical realities; the legislature is supposed to act independently the President, although everyone knows it has no will of its own; e judiciary is supposed to be nonpolitical, although everyone un-rstands that its decisions are guided by political *savoir-faire* rather an principles of jurisprudence. Nevertheless, the forms are ob-rved, even where they seem to the onlooker merely ceremonial: e President proposes legislation, which the parliament goes rough the motions of debating; the court hears evidence and hands wn a learned decision that coincidentally favors the position opted by the President.

Often the divergence between constitutional form and political ality is so great, however, that what occurs politically can simply t be contained within the terms of the fundamental law. When s happens, one does not simply violate the constitution; he re-ites it, to extend the dignity of constitutionality to the new situa-n. Normally, the dictator who wants to have a second term as Pres-ent, when the constitution limits him to one, calls a constitutional nvention to produce a new document; a successful revolution tifies itself retroactively by writing itself a new constitution; and on. In any case, the successful revolution that is more than a sim-palace revolt will want to provide itself with a new constitution embody its principles in the nation's basic law. This signalizes the nge in national orientation that has taken place, and is perfectly ical in the light of the meaning of revolution developed in the ceding pages.

An interesting variation on this theme occurs in Mexico, where the constitution, but the organization and statutes of the ruling

Revolutionary party, have twice been reshaped with the accession power of a new "strong President," representing a new politi tendency. Since Calles founded the party as the PNR (National R olutionary Party) in 1928, it has been reorganized twice, in 1938 Lázaro Cárdenas as the PRM (Party of the Mexican Revolution) the wave of nationalist feeling following the expropriation of the f eign oil companies, and by incoming President Miguel Alemán the PRI (Party of Revolutionary Institutions) in 1946, symbolizi the party's coming to maturity and its swing to the Right.

AMENDMENT AND SUSPENSION OF CONSTITUTIONAL PROVISIONS

One might expect to find relatively easy processes of constitutio amendment, but this is not always the case. Amendment of the c stitution, in every case, requires more than the simple plurality of t legislature necessary for the passage of ordinary law. At the le passage of the amendment by the national Congress must occur two occasions, separated by a decent enough interval that the pub can be presumed to have had a chance to debate the amendm thoroughly. This is the rule in Peru and Ecuador. Congressional tion on the amendment, too, always must be taken by an exceptio majority—not just a plurality of those voting, but a majority or e two-thirds of the total number of legislators. The requirement fo special convention to approve the amendment in addition to an firmative vote of the Congress is common. Finally, the federal s tem of Mexico, in addition, assigns the state legislature, as w as the national Congress, a voice in the amendment process.

Even though the formal processes of amendment may seem present obstacles to innovation, these obstacles, like those of the di sion of powers, can of course be overcome by a political movem that enjoys substantial support, and very little difficulty seems have been experienced in fact in the amending of constitutions

Amending the constitution, or more frequently, scrapping it a replacing it with his own, is a project high on the priority list of dictator, regardless of how he comes to power. Even where he w a free election and controls a majority of the legislature, provisi a democratic constitution are likely to erect impediments to the ›ooth functioning of a dictatorship (although not as many as one ›ght suppose, as will appear in the discussion of the Executive be- ›v). The first target for amendment is invariably the prohibition the immediate re-election of the President, which is almost uni- ›rsal in Latin America.

Another aspect of the fact that constitutions are not the sacrosanct ›cuments that one might expect is that typically the Latin Ameri- ›n constitution itself permits the suspension of some of its pro- ›ions under emergency conditions. These are most commonly the ›ovisions giving individuals immunity from arbitrary arrest and ›tention, and guaranteeing the political freedoms—speech, press, ›d assembly. These can be suspended—temporarily, although tem- ›rary emergencies have a way of dragging out—on the declaration a state of siege, which is made by the President but normally, ›ough not always, requires the concurrence of the legislative body; ›is designed to be used in cases of foreign invasion, armed insurrec- ›n, and the like, but is generally used whenever opposition to the ›vernment seems likely to take a violent turn.

Uruguay is alone among the Latin American republics in having ›constitution that makes no provision for a state of siege, although ›e Costa Rican constitution places heavy restrictions on the Presi- ›nt's siege powers. While the stage of siege is supposed to be lim- ›d in time to the period of the emergency itself, it often happens ›at the declaration is renewed each time it expires, and any given ›esident may govern during the greater part of his term under ›te-of-siege conditions. Thus, "constitutional dictatorship" becomes ›ssible, and many good democrats—like President Betancourt of ›enezuela—have found themselves forced by circumstances to sus- ›nd constitutional guarantees repeatedly. On the other hand, the ›te of siege device is more often used by authoritarian dictators to ›eserve a façade of legality for their regimes; using the state-of-siege ›ovision, a President may be a notorious tyrant without violating ›e law in a technical sense.

B. THE LEGISLATURE

ORGANIZATION

In form, the Latin American legislature resembles the legislatu of continental Europe, modified by the addition of features simil to characteristics of the United States Congress.

The national legislatures each have two chambers, except for Par guay and five out of the six Central American states.[2] The upp chamber (in every case, called the Senate) is always smaller than t lower (the Chamber of Deputies or Chamber of Representatives and its members have longer terms of office. Accordingly, membe ship in the Senate is always more prestigious than belonging to t Chamber.[3] In Argentina, Brazil, and Chile, senatorial terms a staggered—that is, only part of the Senate is renewed at each electi —as is the case in the United States. Elsewhere all Senators a elected simultaneously.

POLITICAL SIGNIFICANCE

Normally, the national Congress follows the President's lead, a proving government bills and facilitating in other ways the gover ment's performance of its functions. For most purposes, one ca regard the policies followed by a Latin American country as t President's policies. There have been, however, numerous exceptio to this rule, and legislatures do pursue an independent line on c casion.[4]

Of the independent power of the Latin American legislature, o could say in general that it varies inversely with the politic

[2] Guatemala, Honduras, El Salvador, Costa Rica, and Panama—all exce Nicaragua, in other words.

[3] With the possible exception of Brazil.

[4] Of course in most countries of the world the government dominates t legislature, the United States Congress (especially the Senate) being one of t few surviving instances of a legislative body that actually writes the countr legislation itself. North Americans should accordingly be wary of treating th own national legislature as the normal case from which to measure deviatio it is actually highly exceptional.

ɾength of the President, and directly with the number of parties ›litically active. The first relationship is clear enough; the more the ·esident controls the conduct of affairs, the less anyone else does, ıd *vice versa.* As to the second: the legislature can most assert its ›litical independence of the President where a multi-party system ·ists, because in a two-party system, and certainly in a single-party stem, the President's authority with the members of his own party ill usually suffice to provide him with a majority in the legistive branch. Where the President's party is but one among several, ›wever, he is more constrained to compromise with parliamentary aders from groups other than his own to try to get their assent to s program, in which in any case he may fail. It is probably in Chile ıd Brazil, countries with continuing multi-party systems, that the ·esident experiences the greatest difficulty in securing legislative ·pport, although the national legislatures in Colombia and Ven-;uela frequently prove intractable; but legislative "rebellions" ;ainst the President's leadership have been known to occur in all e republics except those with overwhelming single-party control the legislature.[5]

It is interesting to note that where the paths of President and legisture do diverge today, the legislature normally takes a position flecting the special interests of individual groups in the society, the resident's position being more in consonance with the interest of .e nation as a whole. This difference in orientation between the two ·gans of state authority is becoming more notable today when the ·publics are being faced with the necessity of taking action to proote economic development which, while in the long-run interest . the nation, certainly damages the interests of specific economic ·oups in the short run. This problem will be taken up at greater ngth later, in the discussion of policy issues. At this point, however, e may note several interesting features of this emerging divergence ı orientation.

One feature is that the defense of group interests by members of

[5] At the time of writing, Mexico, Bolivia, Paraguay, Nicaragua, and Haiti. he Cuban government currently functions without a formal legislature.

the legislature extends to the whole range of interests embraced b the country's economy. Most often it is still the interests of th wealthier sections of the community that find especial representatio in the Congress. That is, "legislative rebellions" today take plac typically over a land reform program that damages landowner i terests or over the introduction, extension, or enforcement of a income tax law. This is to be expected in a class society in whic the upper social groups are inevitably over-represented in the legi lature (sometimes to the virtual exclusion of the lower) by virtu of their wealth, professional skills, and family connections.

However, it also happens that portions of a President's prograr that adversely affect the interests of wage-earners likewise engende legislative opposition, and a freeze in wages or a reduction in th number of civil service employees is just as unlikely to pass th Congress as a graduated income tax.

This situation is directly comparable to that in the United State where the President has a national constituency and conceives c himself as acting in the interests of all the people, whereas the men bers of Congress are responsible primarily to districts in which sp cific interests predominate.

It is interesting to note that this situation differs from what th partisans of Presidency and legislature 100 years ago expected woul evolve. In Latin America, as in the United States, the strong Pres dency was regarded then as a bulwark of privilege and the *statu quo,* whereas the popular house of the legislature was expected t represent the interests of the less affluent members of society. Th expectation need not be exactly reversed today, but nearly so.

FUNCTIONS AND POWERS

The powers of the legislatures may be divided, for convenienc into three categories: legislative, censorial, and electoral.

The legislative functions are what one would expect; the parli ment passes bills and resolutions. In addition, it approves or rejec proposed amendments to the constitution, although, as noted abov extraordinary majorities and in some cases special conventions ar uired. One should note that almost always the Congress acts on islative drafts originating elsewhere, usually with the President d the cabinet; the Congress passes upon legislation, but does not tiate it.

The censorial functions of the parliament are those in the permance of which it acts as a watchdog or controller of the Execue. In the first place, the legislature may impeach the President d usually cabinet members and judicial officers. Where the legisure is bicameral, the standard arrangement is for the Chamber impeach and the Senate to try, as in the United States. This power rarely invoked, although it can be used by a dictator in the process consolidating his power to remove the possibility of judicial opsition to his rule. Perón's controlled legislature, for example, moved the entire Argentine Supreme Court when it struck down vernment legislation as unconstitutional.

Normally, the Congress must approve the declaration of a state siege, and sometimes has the power of disapproving actions taken the President under his siege powers. It also often has the power review and nullify decrees issued by the President.

In about half a dozen of the republics the legislature has the nstitutional power of voting its lack of confidence in a member the President's cabinet, who must then resign. This is a curious ovision to find in a Presidential system, and can only be based on misunderstanding of how such a system necessarily operates, since e President always sets the general direction of policy and *he* ed not resign on a vote of "no confidence." To make one of his inisters resign, therefore, does not necessarily induce a change in e orientation of government policy; the President may simply d someone else to take over its implementation. To deny the legisure's confidence to one of the President's ministers can certainly used in a guerrilla war against the President; but the ministers main responsible to him, and not to the Congress.

Where provisions designed to enforce the responsibility of the binet to the Congress have been introduced, they have foundered the Gibraltar of Presidential power, power not only legal in that it stems from provisions of the constitution, but also political in tl a popularly elected President can count on public support far mo than can the leaders of the legislature. Attempts to introduce ca net responsibility in an otherwise Presidential system have uniforn led at best to failure, at worst to disaster. What they promote is, effect, a running battle between the President and the Congress ov control of the cabinet—for no strong President can simply surrenc control of the cabinet to the legislature: he needs it to carry throu his program and to perform successfully his role as head of t national administration.

This metaphoric war became a quite literal war in Chile, in 18 when President Balmaceda tried to recover the authority over t cabinet that the constitution conferred on the President but tl previous holders of the office had been content to relinquish to t national legislature. The war ended in a parliamentary victory a Balmaceda's suicide.

In 1947, in a similar showdown between President and Congre Cuban President Grau San Martín broke an attempt to impleme the parliamentary control of the cabinet that had been written i the constitution, by simply re-appointing to another cabinet pos minister who had resigned after losing a vote of confidence in t Congress.

In view of experience to date with the attempt to introduce p liamentary responsibility of the cabinet into the Presidential syste it is clear that such semi-parliamentary systems are not viable.[6] T most recent attempt in this direction was made in Brazil in 1961 a abrogated with overwhelming popular support after sixteen mon of indecision, confusion, and frustration. Responsibility of cabinet legislature has been workable in Latin America only under t Uruguayan collegial system abolished in 1966.

Similar observations might be made of Congress's power to co firm, or deny confirmation to, Presidential appointees to high po

[6] This has also been demonstrated in France, where the Fifth Repub semi-parliamentary façade thinly disguises a benevolent Presidential dicta ship.

ɩd to the upper military ranks. It is a power over specific persons ɩt not over the direction of policy.

Of particular interest among other miscellaneous censorial powers the power of the Uruguayan and Chilean legislatures to appoint ɩditors, responsible to them, of the national accounts.

In line with the conception of Congress as censor of executive tion is the tradition of a permanent commission, or committee, of ɔngress that functions during the period in which Congress is not session, exercising Congress's powers of review of executive acts.

The electoral functions of the national Congresses are of two pes: those which involve Congress's acting as a tribunal to pass ɩ the validity of elections, and those in which Congress itself elects dividuals to office. As an electoral tribunal, the Congress will perrm various ceremonial operations in connection with the election the President, but, more importantly, is the sole judge of the ɪalifications of its own members. That is, the outcome of a disɩted election for legislative office can only be decided by the naɔnal legislature itself. Now clearly a Congress is not an impartial gan that will make determinations of this kind solely on the basis the validity of the arguments on either side. It is unlikely, in other ɔrds, that the members of a party that has won a seat by fraud e going to vote against the party's retaining the seat, simply be.use of procedural irregularities alleged to be involved. It is much ore likely that each legislator will vote in such a manner as to vor his own party, regardless of where the merits of the case lie.[7] his is especially so since in many disputed elections illegal actives can be shown to have been conducted on behalf of all the ndidates. Thus, after each Congressional election in Mexico the ɩblic is regaled with endless tales of corrupt election practices and utual recriminations among the parties, during the period in hich the national legislature sits as an electoral tribunal. At the

[7] It seems to me that this occurs to a greater extent in Latin America, premably because of the attitudes discussed in the previous chapters, than it ɩes in the countries of Western Europe, where similar rules apply.

conclusion of the proceedings in the case of each disputed electio the legislative body votes on which candidate should be seated. B to verify the welter of charges that are made would occupy so mu time, and would so frequently entail, in all likelihood, the disqua fication of all the candidates, that in actuality the majority part the PRI, votes in each case to confirm its own candidate (for who inevitably the popular majority has been reported) in his seat, wi the merest handful of seats being allowed the opposition partie These are universally regarded as being in the nature of consolati prizes to the opposition, rather than as indicating that the candida in question has actually the best title to be seated.

In addition to this indifferently performed role of electoral t bunal, the Congress itself acts for some purposes as an elector college. In the dozen states without an elected Vice-President, Co gress chooses the successor to a President who dies in office, retir or who is unable to discharge his functions. This person (or p sons) may be designated in advance, on the beginning of a ne Presidential term; they will then be known, in the order in whi they are to succeed, as First *Designado,* Second *Designado,* and on. The title of *Designado* carries with it no duties, in contrast the office of Vice-President, which normally entails presiding ov the Senate. Alternatively, the President's successor may be designat only when the need has actually arisen. Then, often the pers chosen will act as Provisional President only, until a new popul election can be organized. In the interim between the death or resi nation of the President and the meeting of Congress called to pi his successor, the constitutional officer specified in the constituti itself—say, the President of the Supreme Court, often picked by t constitutional fathers as the least likely to try to perpetuate hims in office[8]—will serve as Provisional President.

If the constitution requires a stipulated percentage[9] of the p ular vote for the election of a President (which no candidate m receive where several candidates are running) then the Congress

[8] Too hopefully, experience has repeatedly shown.
[9] For example, in Honduras, 50 per cent; in Peru, 33.3 per cent.

empowered to choose a President from the leading candidates. In such a case, it is likely simply to pick the candidate who gained most popular votes—he will probably be uttering dire threats should the choice fall on one of his rivals, which may or may not have any effect. Of course it may happen that the legislators are unable to agree on a single choice; a legislative deadlock at such a time, however, is simply an invitation to a *coup d'état,* as Honduran experience has demonstrated.[10]

C. THE EXECUTIVE

THE POLITICAL SIGNIFICANCE OF THE LATIN AMERICAN PRESIDENT

In every country of Latin America with the sole exception of Cuba, the President dominates the nation's government and politics. A glance at the political position of the President, and then at his legal powers, will show why this is necessarily the case.

Today, in all the republics except, temporarily, Brazil, the President is elected by popular vote. Electoral colleges in Peru, Argentina, Chile, and Cuba have been abolished within the last generation, and the power of electing the President taken from the hands of Congress in Haiti. (The military rulers of Brazil in 1966 preferred their candidate to be "elected" by a docile Congress, rather than risk a popular vote.) The President thus enjoys the personal popularity and authority that will cause his office to predominate over its rivals, irrespective of other factors. This is especially the case, as was noted previously, when the weakness of loyalties to institutional processes and political parties causes political life to center around personalities.

In addition, as one man, the President easily holds a more commanding position than the Congress, where party in-fighting and the general stereotype of parliament as a place where only useless debating is done weaken the legislature in popular eyes. Moreover, the President is the undisputed head, as a general rule, of his political

[10] The latest instance of a *coup*'s taking place in Honduras when no candidate had a clear majority occurred in the fall of 1954.

party. This is likely to give him control of Congress; and frequently legislators are elected solely on the basis of their loyalty to the President or the Presidential candidate.

In his capacity as head of the Executive Branch, the President finds himself with many potent means of influencing opinion in his favor at hand. In a leading position is the patronage weapon, which plays a key role in Latin American politics. Furthermore, the discretion in the interpretation and application of the laws normally falling to the executive can be used to great effect to align political forces in the President's favor; export licenses and government bank loans can be withheld or granted; a projected road can pass this way or that; one scheduled irrigation project can be given priority over another; and so on.

Reinforcing, and being reinforced by, these political strengths of the President, there are also the considerable legal powers that normally attach to the office, which go much beyond those at the disposal of the United States President. The power to declare a state of siege has already been discussed; it enables the President, with the consent of the Congress if Congress is in session, to establish a temporary dictatorship and suspend individual freedoms, where the survival of the constitutional order is endangered. Of course this power lends itself to abuse, although conditions that do justify the imposition of a state of siege are in fact often present.

The power to issue decrees having the force of law also lies at the disposition of the President. Decree powers are known to all modern constitutions—even the United States has its executive orders, and Britain its Orders-in-Council—but their legitimate scope varies a great deal from one country to another. In the Latin American republics, the President's constitutional power of *reglamento,* the power to issue regulations necessary to supply gaps in Acts of the legislature, may be used to enact supplementary legislation. Presidential lawmaking on important questions occurs with much greater frequency, however, on the basis of delegations of power from the Congress authorizing the President to issue decrees on specific matters for specific periods, or under emergency decree-making powers that become available automatically on the declaration of a state of siege.

The President's powers over the spending of money are greater than those available in the United States (although in recent years the American Presidency has moved in the Latin American direction in some respects). Quite frequently the President, using his decree powers, can divert funds from one budgetary category to another, or he can even incur expenses over the budgetary allocation.

Finally, in the three federal states, the President has the power, in effect, of "firing" state governors and replacing them with his own appointees, although in Brazil this occurs infrequently under democratic Presidents. In Mexico, the federal Senate has the power of appointing a new governor where it finds that the constitutional authorities of the state have disappeared. No stringent definition of such a situation exists, and, normally, political criteria prevail, the Senate following the President's lead. In Argentina and Brazil the leading ground for the appointment of a federal "interventor" is in order to maintain a republican form of government (a phrase borrowed from the U. S. Constitution)—a very elastic contingency. Other grounds are provided, but are seldom needed. Presidents have used decree powers to "intervene" other institutions, even private ones, such as labor unions or business firms, in similar fashion.

Perhaps one should add that, even with respect to the powers that the Latin American President shares with the United States President, he enjoys a more potent position. For example, his powers in relation to the legislative process are similar: he recommends laws, and can veto them. But in the majority of Latin American states, not only can the President propose laws, but the Congress will leave the drafting and introduction of legislation exclusively to the President. In almost every case, Congress has no legislative drafting office or legislative reference service that would enable it regularly to be the source of the legislative drafts on which it must pass, even if it were so disposed.

LIMITING THE POWERS OF THE PRESIDENCY

As can be seen from the preceding discussion, for most purposes one can consider a country's actions and policies as, in effect, those of the President. In fact, there occur cases in which, because of the amplitude of the legal powers of the President, and the preponderant role that even the most zealously constitutional President plays, it is an open question whether a given Chief Executive is a dictator or simply a strong constitutional President. We shall revert to this question when we come to consider Presidential dictatorship.

Because it is relatively easy, by overusing the powers legally available to him, for the President to tyrannize over the country, attempts have been made to limit the legal authority of the Presidency. We have already seen that the institution of cabinet responsibility to the legislature does not limit the President's pre-eminence, but instead impels him to abrogate the constitutional prerogatives of the parliament in order to play his accustomed role.

Occasionally, a President may allow a Prime Minister to be the actual director of policy, but no popularly-elected President need find himself under any compulsion to do so. One recent instance in which a Prime Minister was indeed allowed a wide range of authority was that of Pedro Beltrán of Peru, appointed to the office by President Manuel Prado, who (passing into his seventies halfway through his term) was no longer interested in maintaining a firm grip on the reins of policy in a situation in which economic circumstances called for drastic and unpopular measures to be taken.

Where a President does not in fact assume the vigorous leadership of affairs, this is likely to occur because of the weakness of a political position resulting from his election by a narrow segment of the electorate in a contest in which none of the several candidates became the overwhelming popular choice. In recent years, this was the case of President Ponce Enríquez of Ecuador, the narrowly elected candidate of a Conservative party[11] that was in a clear mi-

[11] Ponce Enríquez is actually leader of the small Christian Social Party, but was endorsed by the Conservatives and elected by Conservative votes.

ority position in the country. Such a President is able to count on upport neither in the Congress nor among the people.

The most drastic way to limit the powers of the Presidency and nsure against Presidential dictatorship is—to abolish the Presidency ltogether! After pointing out that the two possible types of demo-ratic government are the Presidential, involving a separation of owers (like that of the United States), and the parliamentary, nvolving the fusion of powers in the legislature (Great Britain), ne textbooks have to add the afterthought, or footnote, that Switzer-and has a political system that seems to fall properly in neither ategory: the collegial executive. In the Swiss system, which is ather like the commission form of municipal government, an exec-tive council with members chosen for fixed terms collectively heads ne Executive Branch (each member being responsible for a cabinet epartment) and collectively exercises the powers attributed to the hief Executive in a Presidential system.

Under the influence of the great shaper of modern Uruguay, José atlle y Ordóñez, the Uruguayans have experimented with a col-egial executive similar to the Swiss. The *colegiado* system most ecently in effect, that adopted in 1952 and operating from 1954 to 967, differed from the Swiss in several respects, among them that nembers of the National Council in Uruguay did not head execu-ve departments but instead supervised a cabinet whose individual nembers were responsible to the legislature. The *colegiado* suc-eeded far too well in its mission of diluting executive power as a way f avoiding dictatorship, however. Council seats were assigned on ne basis of four to the major faction of the major party, two to s second-largest faction, and three to the minority party. As a esult of this provision and other divisive practices which arose, ne Council was weakened to the point that it could not take de-sive action with respect to the country's problems, which steadily ecame more acute, especially in the economic realm. Eventually it ecame impossible, even for many former partisans of the *colegiado* ystem, to overlook its contribution to the general deterioration in ne country's condition, and the plural executive was abolished in the elections of November, 1966. The Uruguayans simultaneously made clear their desire for strong government by electing a retired general as first president under the new unipersonal system.

One method that all the republics, with the sole exception, today of the dictatorships of Haiti, Cuba, and Paraguay, have adopted to limit the evolution of the constitutional President into a dictator, is to stipulate that no President can succeed himself in office. In most of the republics an ex-President may be re-elected to the office after "skipping" a term, however, and it is common for ex-Presidents to make comebacks. In the last decade ex-Presidents Vargas (Brazil), Ibáñez del Campo (Chile), Velasco Ibarra (Ecuador), Betancourt (Venezuela), Prado (Peru), Paz Estenssorro (Bolivia), and Lleras Camargo (Colombia) have all returned to the Presidency after a lapse of time. For example, two of the candidates in the Costa Rican Presidential elections of 1962 were ex-Presidents, as were all three of the candidates in the Dominican elections of 1966.

PRESIDENTAL DICTATORSHIP

Usurpation of the President's Office. Given the prohibition of immediate re-election as a guarantee against the erection of a dictatorship, it follows that the President who would make himself a dictator—with occasional curious exceptions—must somehow circumvent this provision. In abrogating the prohibition of re-election or in offering himself for re-election, a President thus crosses the Rubicon and takes leave of generally accepted constitutional norms no matter how careful he has been up to that point to secure a legal façade for his actions by procuring Congressional grants of delegated legislative powers, and the like.

The sharp break with the constitutional tradition entailed in the violation of the prohibition of re-election is the kind of act that would-be dictators try to avoid, as it only serves to strengthen and consolidate the opposition and alienate the uncommitted. To the maximum extent possible, the dictator tries to contain his act within the bounds of legality—for the sake of administrative coherence and the obtaining of a good press abroad, as well as to avoid unnecessary lomestic opposition. A great deal of rewriting and amending of con-titutions is invested in this effort, of course. Consider the case of 3etúlio Vargas: coming to power at the head of a revolt in 1930, he uled as "Provisional President" until 1934; in that year a constitu-ional convention rewrote the nation's fundamental law, terminating ts work by electing Vargas the first "Constitutional President" to erve under its provisions; toward the end of his term, in 1937, 'argas staged a *coup d'état,* abrogated the 1934 constitution, and lecreed a new one, which remained legally in effect, though honored nore in the breach than the observance, until he was forced to resign he Presidency in 1945.

In point of fact, the expiration of his term of office is always a ime of crisis for the dictator-President. Normally, he attempts to ontinue in the office himself; sometimes, he merely tries to impose is own choice as successor; occasionally, a dictator will preside over elatively free elections to choose the man to succeed him—Batista id this in 1944, for example, Odría in 1956. In the first two types f situation, revolts are frequent, made before the election by the pposition or by a member of the ruling group passed over for the egime's nomination, or after the election by a defeated candidate harging fraud, or by a populace disgusted with the travesty on emocratic procedures they have witnessed. In Mexico of the 1920s, or example, revolts accompanied, immediately preceded, or im-nediately followed the Presidential elections of 1920, 1924, 1928, and 929 (the last for Provisional President, following the assassination f the President-elect). Similarly, United States intervention in Cuba nder the terms of the Platt Amendment, to ensure the continuation f constitutional processes, occurred during the revolts and attendant ivil wars that followed the Presidential elections of 1906, 1912, and 916.

The wise dictator, cognizant of the problem of the re-election risis, finds ways of short-circuiting the crisis period, or tries to. 'robably the most successful method is the one used by Vargas in 934—to call a constituent convention that itself elects the dictator o the first term under the provisions of the new document that it drafts. This circumvents the popular agitation to which an election campaign gives rise, and indeed does not even allow the crystallization of opinion around rival candidates. Maximilian Hernández Martínez of El Salvador executed this maneuver twice, having constituent assemblies elect him to a new term in 1939 and again in 1944.

An original device to secure his continuance in office was contrived in 1961 by President Duvalier of Haiti. Duvalier had his name printed at the head of the ballot for members of Congress for the legislative elections occurring halfway through the six-year Presidential term, and then announced that he had been re-elected President for a new term without opposition.

The danger that an election too obviously and heavy-handedly rigged can create for the dictator is illustrated by the fate of Pérez Jiménez in Venezuela. The dictator's henchmen organized a plebiscite in place of the election scheduled for 1957, with voters able to deposit a "Yes" or "No" card indicating whether or not they favored the continuance of Pérez Jiménez in office. Various techniques were adopted to ensure that the outcome would be favorable to the regime —for example, government employees (who form a substantial proportion of the population) were required to report for work on the day following the election with their "No" cards, as evidence that they had not been cast, resident foreigners were allowed to vote,[12] and so on. General popular disgust with the whole farce contributed directly to the military *coup* that unseated Pérez Jiménez shortly after the "plebiscite." The dictator might have had better luck if he had relied on the maneuver used at the election of the constitutional assembly that first named him to the Presidency five years before. Then the military *junta* ruling the nation had simply announced a set of election results in conformity with its wishes, although not with the votes cast, after preliminary returns had suggested that the election was going "the wrong way."

[12] Venezuela has large numbers of residents of Spanish and Italian origin especially. Under United States law U. S. citizens may forfeit their citizenship for voting in a foreign election, however.

There are three types of methods an incumbent administration an use to "rig" elections so as to continue itself in office. The first, hich consists simply of falsifying the returns, already has been ted. By this technique it is possible to achieve a favorable outcome ven where opposition parties may campaign freely and voters may ast their ballots as they choose. Difficulties for this approach may e presented, however, by demands of the opposition parties to be epresented on election tribunals and in the process of tallying the ote. Nevertheless, what might be called arithmetical fraud is quite idespread in Latin America (it is not unknown elsewhere!), and ven where the national government itself attempts to conduct an onest election it occurs at the local level.

An incumbent government can also influence the outcome of an lection in which the votes are fairly counted, by throwing the eight of its official powers behind the regime's own candidate. erhaps this technique reached its maximum effectiveness under erón, whose election victories were apparently genuine ones in an rithmetical sense. Perón's government would allow opposition candidates, but would subject them to extreme harassment and make impossible for them to campaign. Opposition newspapers were losed under various pretexts, the use of the radio was denied opponents of the regime, and so on.

Finally, often elections are held with only a single candidate competing. The attractiveness of democratic ideals, however much belied y dictatorial realities, remains so great that authoritarian governments feel that even this type of "election" confers a measure of gitimacy. The regime may have outlawed all candidacies save the fficial one, or opposition parties may have boycotted the election ecause they knew the vote would not be counted fairly in any case although sometimes opposition parties stage a boycott and make his charge simply to save face when they know they would stand o chance in a fairly tallied vote).

By one means or another, *imposición,* the imposition on the voters f an "official" candidate, regardless of their preferences, is a general ractice. In the entire history of several of the republics no Presidential candidate sponsored by the incumbent administration has ever been defeated in a popular election. This has on occasion been because he was in reality the popular choice, of course.

Because of the prevalence of *imposición,* it is not enough to assume that a President who traces his title to a popular election is a legitimate democrat, whereas one who came to power through a revolt is a dictatorial usurper. The popular election in question may have been thoroughly rigged, whereas the revolt may have been a genuine expression of the popular will, forced to take the path of revolt because it had been frustrated by the corruption of the electoral process. Woodrow Wilson's policies with respect to Latin America frequently came to grief because of his failure to understand this point.

Dictatorial Government. The medievals, who had much experience with tyrants, and, especially because of religious scruples, wished to be clear at what point they were justified in withholding their allegiance from a ruler or conspiring to overthrow him, used to distinguish between the tyrant by usurpation, the ruler who had no legitimate claim to his position, and the tyrant by performance, who may have had a legitimate claim, but forfeited it by his conduct in office.

This distinction can be suggestive for our present purposes. The tyrant by usurpation, the President who owes his sash of office to a *coup d'état* or a falsified election, has certainly no legitimate title and thus provides a sufficient ground for honorable men to oppose him. It is possible, on the other hand, for a President to command popular support and to win election after election and be a tyrant nevertheless. This is a point that was often lost sight of in the disputes over the ambiguous character of the government of Fidel Castro that took place during 1961, with one side arguing that, as he refused to hold elections, he was a dictator, the other that elections were divisive and wasteful, and in any case unnecessary since Fidel obviously had majority support. There are things beside elections that determine whether or not a man is a dictator, after all.

Discussion of this point should not rest simply on the postulation of a dichotomy between democracies and dictatorships. Actually, considerable variations are possible within the category "dictatorship." When we discussed the role of the army in politics, for example, we distinguished between the dictatorship which was of the army, by the army, and for the army, as it were, and the *personal* dictatorship of a leader who happened to be a professional soldier.

One of the simplest, and yet one of the most helpful, ways of distinguishing among dictatorships is to consider how dictatorial they actually are—that is, to introduce the notion of different degrees of dictatorship. This is clearly a factor of central importance to the person who lives under the dictator, and may justifiably influence one's moral evaluation of the system. Although both were surely dictators, for example, there was a world of difference between the rule of Getúlio Vargas, which was on the whole a mild and easy-going authoritarianism, and the institutionalized reign of terror of a gangster such as Trujillo. It is interesting to note that the dictators themselves are rather sensitive about differences of this kind. It was reported of the late Anastasio Somoza of Nicaragua—not himself a particularly benevolent ruler—that he resented the tactics used by Trujillo as tending to give "strong Executive rule" a bad name, and he used to object strenuously to being classified with the Dominican tyrant. General Stroessner of Paraguay, similarly, took pains to point out the differences between himself and Trujillo, laying stress on his claim that he "never had a man killed" except for armed rebels who died fighting against his government.

Completely totalitarian government, absolute dictatorship over every political and social institution—government, army, university, Church—and over every act and utterance of every citizen, is not achieved immediately, of course. The dictator who would be totalitarian engages in a continuing series of political battles with every source of potential opposition until he can feel sure that he rules alone and unchallenged. Of course, he can never be perfectly sure, and the secret political police must be continually busy. The career of Perón is instructive in this regard: in successive skirmishes the unions, the army, the judiciary, and the universities were "co-ordinated" with the regime; Perón fell in the struggle to establish his mastery over the navy and over the Church.

As C. W. Cassinelli has pointed out, totalitarian rule is necessarily personal rule. The totalitarian dictator maximizes his power by sharing it with no one; he balances his party off against the army against the Church perhaps, against the unions, against the officials of government; perhaps only his secret police wields independent power, and it is itself kept in a continual state of turmoil. The stage of secret police domination of the state is thus also the period of maximum deification of the ruler; personalism and terror join hands. This was clearly the case in the heyday of Stalin's rule, and so it was under Trujillo; so it is becoming under Duvalier. The statues of the Leader are erected to the accompaniment of gunfire in the back alleys and screams from the torture chambers.

Few Latin American dictatorships actually become totalitarian—only those of Trujillo, Castro, and Duvalier reached that point with Perón failing in the attempt. For the most part, the Latin American dictator rests content with something less than totalitarian power. It normally suffices him if his orders are carried out and his government unopposed; in many cases the opposition is permitted a moderate amount of activity, so long as this does not actually threaten the dictator's grip on the apparatus of government Under Vargas, for example, the courts occasionally held his acts unconstitutional and still continued to function unmolested—although he continued with his "unconstitutional" policies as though nothing had happened! Minimal dictatorship of this kind is most likely, however, where the dictator is concerned solely with either feathering his nest to the maximum in the shortest possible time (for example, the first years of Batista's rule after his comeback in 1952) and/or with preserving the *status quo* on behalf of the old ruling classes. The strong ruler interested in putting through a program will ordinarily not be as forbearing with the opposition as Vargas was.

HE CABINET

The single most important fact one should note about the cabinet n any Latin American country is that, as under any strong-President onstitution, it can, politically speaking, only be an appendage to ne Chief Executive. The President necessarily determines the direcion of policy; the cabinet is simply a collection of the President's hief administrative and technical assistants. This is true regardless f what the constitution may say about the parliament's powers with elation to the appointment and dismissal of ministers.

There are occasional exceptions to this general rule, where a Presient is enfeebled by age or sickness, or is simply not an assertive erson, and a leading member of the cabinet comes to dominate ne administration. They are rare, however, and limited to individual ases, for the reason that feeble, shy, or unassertive men are hardly kely to be elected to high office in the first place.

Usually there are about 12 members of the President's cabinet, ith the size of the individual bodies currently ranging from 9 to 4 members. As in the United States, separate agencies and commisons are often established, some continuing on a permanent basis, ith heads who report directly to the President.

Within the cabinet itself, the relative importance and political eight attached to the holders of the various portfolios varies. It is iggestive to regard some cabinet positions as being more "politial," others as more "technical," although of course all are both to me degree. The most "political" members of the cabinet will ormally be the Secretary of *Gobernación* or Interior, the Secretary f War or Defense, the Secretary of the Presidency, where one exists, lus in Mexico and Venezuela the Governor of the Federal District, nd in Honduras the mayor of the capital city, Tegucigalpa, who re also members of the cabinet. These individuals will usually be ne most important in domestic politics, the most influential, and ne most likely prospects for future Presidential candidates.

A special word is in order about the Secretary of *Gobernación,* ho has no exact equivalent in the United States, although his functions resemble those of Ministers of Interior in most countries.[13] Hi responsibilities fall into several categories, encompassing principall the supervision of provincial and local government, the administra tion of elections, and the control of the national police. One can se the reason for his title, Minister of Government—although it migh as well be Minister of Politics since, in an administration so dis posed, he is in a position to manipulate election results, create patronage system in local government tied to the ruling party, an use force against opposition elements. In any case, his job require a great deal of political skill and general *savoir-faire,* and makes hir often the second man in the government, after the President. I several of the republics, in addition, the Interior and Justice port folios are regularly held by a single member of the cabinet.

If the Secretary of *Gobernación* is not the second most importan official of the administration, chances are that that distinction fal to the Minister of Defense (or whatever designation is given th minister who has political responsibility for the army). In 13 of th republics, this is a single Minister of Defense or of the Arme Forces, whereas 3 countries have separate ministers for each ser ice.[14] Argentina has a combined system, not unlike that of th United States, except that the Minister of Defense *and* the Secre taries of State of each armed service all have seats in the cabine Costa Rica and Panama, which have no armed forces as such, hav no cabinet portfolios for military departments; supervision of th national police in each country comes under the jurisdiction of th Minister of *Gobernación.*

The political weight of the Minister of Defense varies, of cours with the importance of the army in the country's politics. But eve in the more politically developed states, it is still customary for th minister responsible for the armed forces to be himself a rankin military officer, who is regarded more or less as the representati of service interests.

The Minister for Foreign Affairs is invariably the ranking "tec

[13] In Great Britain, the Home Secretary.

[14] Mexico, with two armed services, and Brazil and Peru, with three.

nical" minister, and is quite often a distinguished figure in the life of his country, a respected scholar, jurist, or man of letters. He is rarely a key party politician, however, and in many countries his ob has almost a non-partisan aura about it. Foreign Ministers become Presidential candidates much less frequently than one might assume from the intrinsic importance of the position, partly because of this factor, partly also because the Minister has usually spent a good deal of time out of the country in lesser diplomatic posts and has not built up a political following; and often because, either as Foreign Minister or in a previous tour of duty as Ambassador to he United States, he came to be regarded as too pro-Yankee.

The portfolios of Education and, sometimes, Justice are generally occupied by similar types, the distinguished professor or jurist who s not really a party politician. Frequently, when a vacancy occurs o head the Foreign Office it is the Minister of Education who is promoted.

HE PUBLIC SERVICE

In the modern state, the public service, ideally, is supposed to be olitically neutral, to confine itself to technical administrative tasks within the policy guidelines established by the country's elected political leadership. To insulate civil servants from political interference, nd to eliminate partisanship in the staffing of non-political posi-ons, holders of bureaucratic office are given security of tenure, eing liable to dismissal only for grave faults, and then only after rigorous procedure has been followed. This security of tenure acts, n addition, to attract candidates of ability to the public service; re-ruitment—again, ideally—depends solely on merit, as tested by ompetitive entrance examination.

Clearly, the merit system can work as it should only under certain ecial social and political conditions. Security of tenure can best be sured in a polity that is stable and commands general popular pport; where the accession of a new leadership to power does not nply a change of policy so great that holders of administrative fice under the previous regime must be assumed to be disloyal to the new one. To go a step further, one might say that the merit system works best in a classless society, where general equality of opportunity in education means that civil service examinations discriminate only on the basis of ability and not on social class.

Viewed in this perspective, it is clear that for the most part the states of Latin America are not well equipped to have modern bureaucracies working for them. They are a long way from equality of opportunity in education; frequent turmoil provides an unfavorable setting for security in tenure; low standards of political morality undermine principles of merit recruitment and tenure—in cases known to the writer, offices have actually been sold: one received an appointment on payment of a fee. Moreover, the tradition of personalism makes it likely that loyalties will be to individual political leaders, not to abstract institutions.

It is possible to argue that, in their present stage of development, a merit bureaucracy would not be functional in view of the needs of most of the Latin American states. From the point of view of the leader who has just come to power, for example, merit or seniority may be of secondary importance to loyalty as a consideration in making key appointments. This is certainly the case if the country has a tradition of violent change of government. Often a President who left in office the functionaries of his predecessor's regime had cause to regret it—Francisco I. Madero, for example, who was deposed and shot by a military commander he should have replaced when he came to power.

One might argue, further, that a spoils system of appointment might have advantages if it were used to create enduring parties in those countries where at present parties are fluctuating personalist groupings. A very good case against a merit bureaucracy could be made, too, in the light of the colossal problems that face Latin American governments: security of tenure makes for complacency, devotion to routine, unimaginativeness, lack of initiative, whereas the obstacles to social development in the Latin American states can be surmounted, if at all, only by individuals chosen for their devotion to the programs and goals of the government leaders.

Despite the difficulties and the negative arguments, however, at- npts have been made to introduce elements of a modern system public administration to some of the countries of the area. Today, least some features of the merit system can be found in nearly . the republics. Some states—most notably Brazil and Costa Rica— ve established central personnel agencies, which set common neral policies; but the general rule is that recruiting and promo- ·n policies are set by each agency for its own personnel, and not a government-wide basis. This makes a certain amount of sense, it results in inequalities and budgetary difficulties of all sorts, in ldition to making bribery and kick-backs harder to eliminate. As result, the merit system comes soonest to those agencies—for ex- nple, the public health services—which perform the most technical sks, for which qualifications over and above the ties of personal iendship and family relationship are clearly required.

A crucial problem is that one of the features of the merit system security of tenure—is readily adopted without the simultaneous loption of the provisions that complement it, or in polities whose her characteristics lend no support to the development of a mod- n bureaucracy. Regulations protecting tenure are easy to adopt cause they are favored by the civil servants themselves, and also the incumbent administration, which wants to blanket its follow- s into tenure positions before it leaves office. As a result, a new lministration finds that it cannot get rid of the public servants it is inherited. Rather than assuming the unlikely: that they are im- rtial and non-political and can be expected to perform loyally, the w government simply creates a set of new positions, which it then ls with the deserving among its own supporters. Thus, the public rvice swells, the necessary work is spread thinner, and red tape arts to multiply. But this process occurs again with the advent of ch succeeding new government. The end result is that civil service bs become part-time or sinecure positions, which are regarded as ch, and are compensated accordingly. This in turn provides a rther reason for expecting a *mordida,* or petty bribe, from the pless citizen, who must pay it or expect his claim, or request, to be lost from sight forever in the mass of paperwork that clogs th channels of administration. Perhaps the leading victim in Lati America of this ailment—the swollen bureaucracy—is Urugua with Brazil following closely.

It is unlikely that a government can attempt drastic measures t break out of the vicious circle of the over-expanded part-time bu reaucracy, despite its inefficiency and expensiveness. To do so woul be to throw many out of work in a society where unemployment i already too great, to make enemies of educated people living in th capital city, which is hard enough to control at the best of time only, in many cases, to replace the expense of their salaries by ex pense almost as great for pensions and unemployment benefits an other forms of government compensation.

D. THE JUDICIARY

The legal systems of Latin America are comparable to those c the continental European countries, rather than of the countrie where English is spoken, in their form, origins, content, and politica implications.

THE CHARACTER OF THE LAW

The origins of the basic concepts of the legal systems of the are are traceable, ultimately, to Roman law, mediated through coloni law, and through the Napoleonic Code and the Spanish codes base on it, which have been extensively copied in Latin America. Thes concepts often result in rules on matters of substance at varianc with the rules one finds in systems based on the English commo law—on such points as inheritance and the character of propert rights, for instance. Of more importance from the point of view c politics, however, may be the general difference in the structure c the two types of law. The one is "code" law, with the provisior applicable to principal fields systematized into codes, whereas th English system is based on "common" law, essentially the whol array of precedents that represent the decisions of judges in specifi cases dating back over 1,000 years. Many observers have contende at the differences between the two types of legal system result in ifferences of habits of mind among lawyers that in turn affect the yle of political life. Under a common law system, it has been gued, students are trained to regard the law as flexible, and matter r argument; they are taught by the case method, which induces agmatism and inductive modes of thought; while the courts use e adversary method of pleading cases (Smith *versus* Doe), which omotes open-mindedness and an acceptance of the legitimacy of iffering points of view. Under the "code" system (the argument es on), the existence of the sum total of valid law in codified form omotes a closed-minded and dogmatic approach; legal instruction resses deductive reasoning and a reliance on authority not con-uctive to democratic attitudes; this is fortified in turn by the more stricted role allowed counsel, and the greater latitude given the dge, in proceedings under the codes. Although influences of this btle a character are hard to trace specifically, it seems reasonable at they have been active at least to some extent in helping to shape e political culture of the Latin states.

One should note that there have been United States influences in me areas of Latin American law—especially on constitutional law, nce institutions modeled on those of the United States have found eir way into the political system. In the federal systems, for ex-nple, precedents of U. S. courts are cited in support of judicial ecisions on federal questions. It is doubtful, however, that many rrowings from the common-law countries can be successfully ab-rbed into systems of law of such basically different character. The ry system, for example, has been tried intermittently, but in gen-al found to work badly; juries are reluctant to convict, for one ing, perhaps because of a different traditional attitude toward ithority.

IE POLITICAL STANDING OF THE JUDICIARY

Invariably, the constitution establishes the judiciary as an inde-endent organ, standing on an equal footing with executive and gislature. The political reality is at variance with the constitutional norm, however, and the courts have a relatively limited sphere (political action in relation to the executive, although in most cas they play a more independent role than does the legislature.

The degree of independence the judges have depends, in the fir instance, on their freedom from influence by the executive. Th depends in turn primarily on their security in office; where judici appointments are made for life (or "during good behavior," whic is normally equivalent to a life appointment), judicial decisions ar freer than if the judge has to consider what the effect of his decisio will be on his chances for reappointment or for re-election by th legislature. Judges of the highest court serve indefinite terms i Argentina, Brazil, Chile, Peru, and now in Mexico. Formerly, ir definite terms were the rule in Cuba, too. In addition, judges i Uruguay, Colombia, and Costa Rica can regularly expect to be co firmed in office when their terms expire. Elsewhere, there is gre pressure on judges not to hand down decisions that will be u popular with President and Congress.

It is also true that the degree of discretion available to a judge i less under a code-law system, where, in principle, the code specifi the decision that is to be reached under every possible set of circur stances, than it is under the common law, where a variety of prec dents may exist that allow a judge greater discretion in arriving a his decision. There is nevertheless some latitude within which range of interpretations of the law is possible even under the mo detailed code. Perhaps the sharpest limitation on the role the court can play in politics in the Latin American republics, as contraste with the United States, is that under the typical Latin America constitution itself the President is given so much power that th Supreme Court, interpreting the constitution, can erect few imped ments to his actions.

The courts' powers to decide questions of constitutionality ar limited in another way. A court may find that the application c the law in question to the case in hand would violate the constit tion; but this finding is limited in its effect to the specific case bein tried—it does not nullify the law. In some countries, an uninte ted series of decisions to the same effect will create binding cedent, however: five decisions in Mexico, and three in Colombia, ome types of case.

. final limit on the political significance of the courts is that troversies in several fields, often those most germane to political es, do not come before the regular court system, but before spe- judicial bodies or tribunals. This is generally true in Latin erica with respect to issues relative to elections, for example, to r questions, to questions of administrative jurisdiction, and to questions. For litigation in each of these areas, a separate set of unals frequently exists, operating under different ground rules usually more subject to political influence than the regular court em.

till, the courts do play a certain political role on occasion, espe- ly in the defense of individual rights. Lacking the means of en- ing their decisions, however, they cannot be expected to provide substantial defense against the imposition of tyranny; the fact the milder dictators permit the courts to continue to function mally (Getúlio Vargas, for example) should be regarded not as lence of the strength of the courts, as it has been by some com- ntators, but as an indication of their ultimate political weakness.

E. NATIONAL-LOCAL RELATIONS

ue to the vastness of the territory that most of the Latin Ameri- republics encompass, and the natural barriers to communication exist, local officials inevitably exercise a great deal of discretion, rdless of the legal and constitutional framework within which function. In addition, there is a sort of *mystique* of the "free" nicipality, with its *cabildo* or council regulating local affairs, ch continues to be influential. There has indeed always been a panic tradition of municipal autonomy, although this has been dily reduced in Spanish America, in part by the improvement in munications, with the early days after Independence probably esenting the high point that municipal autonomy has reached.

hree of the Latin American states are federal republics: Mexico,

TABLE II *Major Political Features of the Latin American States*

	Normal Political Role of Military	Party System	Presidential Term	Other Features
Argentina	Intervene	Multi-party	6 years	Weakly federal
Bolivia	Intervene	Fluctuating multi-party	4 years	In transition from single-party dominance
Brazil	Intervene	Two-partyism stipulated by law	5 years	President elected by legislature; federal
Chile	Limited	Multi-party	6 years	Tradition of strong legislature
Colombia	Limited	Conservatives and Liberals (both in factions)	4 years	National Front till 1976: parties share all posts, alternate in Presidency
Costa Rica	None	Multi-party	4 years	Unicameral legislature; many agencies independent of Presidential control
Cuba	Revolutionary army; in control	C.P.C. dominant	Constitution of 1940 though associated with	in suspension; Prime Minister dictator "collective leadership"
Dominican Republic	Intervene	Multi-party	4 years	
Ecuador	Intervene	Fluctuating multi-party	4 years	Some Senators represent functional groups
El Salvador	In control	Emergent multi-party	6 years	Unicameral legislature

Guatemala	Intervene	Multi-party	6 years	Unicameral legislature
Haiti	Veto power	Nebulous	Indefinite	Currently personal dictatorship
Honduras	Intervene	Liberal and Nationalist	6 years	Unicameral legislature
Mexico	Limited	P.R.I. dominant	6 years	Weakly federal
Nicaragua	In control	2 Conservative, 2 Liberal parties	4 years	Somoza family hegemony
Panama	National Police; veto power	Unstable, personalist	4 years	Unicameral legislature
Paraguay	In control	Colorados dominant	5 years; re-eligible	Unicameral legislature; permanent dictatorship
Peru	Intervene	Multi-party	6 years	Cabinet nominally responsible to legislature
Uruguay	Limited	Colorado and Blanco (both in factions)	4 years	Cabinet responsible to legislature
Venezuela	Veto power	Multi-party	5 years	Nominally federal

Argentina, and Brazil, with all the others being unitary stat The formal difference is this: in a federal system, the member-sta of the federation have reserved powers that the federal governme may not assume, and they may act in areas of policy that are f bidden to the federal government. To guarantee their retention their rights under the system, the states must participate in t process of constitutional amendment, certainly if the alteration their own status is contemplated. In the unitary scheme, on t other hand, there may be considerable provincial autonomy, b legally this is only permitted by the central government at pleasure, and does not exist for the provincial government as a rig

One would expect to see a great difference between the unit and the federal systems, then, in the powers concentrated at the le intermediate between national and local government, that of t state, province, or department, corresponding to the different co stitutional-legal principles involved. In actuality, the differences not great. Although Venezuela is officially styled a "federal republi the state governors are actually Presidential appointees, for ample, whereas many constitutions organized along unitary li provide for elected provincial assemblies, and two—those of Cu and Uruguay—envisage an elected provincial executive. In any ca the practice of federal intervention, and the holding of a fede power to intervene in reserve, means in effect that the states Mexico or the provinces of Argentina are not much different powers from the departments of Chile, say. Emilio Portes Gil, former President of Mexico, has frankly called Mexican federali "a great lie." Only in Brazil (except of course for its relatively inf quent periods of dictatorship) can one consistently see states ge inely pursuing courses of action independent of the federal gove ment, and even conflicting with it, with impunity, comparable to w takes place in the North American states or the Canadian provin Brazil has a relatively strong tradition of state autonomy, und standable given the colossal size of the country, which flouris especially in the 40 years between the abdication of the Empe and the accession to power of Getúlio Vargas. Vargas replaced

:cted state governors by his appointees, and ended the inde-
ndence of the states, but it revived thereafter, and until the im-
·sition of military rule in 1965 stood clearly in a different category
›m the position of states in Mexico or Argentina.

Federal intervention, which was referred to above in the section
. the Presidency, is a device under which the federal government
kes over the administration of a state, supplanting state authorities.
he occasions for intervention provided in the constitutions are in
ality interpreted broadly so as to cover any conceivable situation.

IV *Policy*

A. THE MAKING OF POLICY

IN CONSTITUTIONAL states functioning according principles of the separation of powers, one might expect the flow policy in the process of formation to move in a course suggested l the sequence of the topics dealt with to this point: groups-partie legislature-executive-judiciary. In other words, policy could be e pected to originate in the needs of specific population groups, arisi against a background of a given political culture and state of publ opinion; from this starting point should derive the programs, pe sonnel, and policy orientations of the political parties, which, throu the channels of legislative action, frame projects of law to answ those needs; the implementation of the laws approved by the leg lature rests, in turn, with the executive authorities, limited, it m be, by judicial determinations.

The premise that has guided the relative emphasis placed on t different elements in the material this book covers has been bas on a rather different conception of the process of policy-makin Policy, in this view, is set principally in the direct interaction executive (that is, President) and groups; the other agencies th are formally involved in the process play a quite secondary and oft negligible role. The pattern is of this nature: policy is set by t President on the basis of his conception of public needs and personal ideals and goals of his own; it is retracted, modified, extended on the basis of groups' reactions aimed directly at the Pr ident—in "behind the scenes" access to him personally, leading

forts at persuasion, intimidation, or bribery; and in strikes, lock-
uts, demonstrations, riots, and threats of revolution and *coup d'état*.
he role of legislature and judiciary is minimized, that of groups is
ugmented; while the parties serve principally to call the signals for
oup direct action.

Fidel Castro's "direct democracy," his enunciation of new policies
the course of an oration to a sympathetic crowd that shouts ap-
opriate responses, is thus a kind of caricature of the processes by
hich policy is actually made in the countries of the area.

Let us now turn to examine some of the substantive problems of
olicy-making. Because of the evident limitations of space, the dis-
ussion below will be confined to the major policy issue in contempo-
ry Latin America: policy for economic development. The conclud-
g section will tie together some of the major themes developed in
e book in a treatment of "policy for political development."

B. POLICY FOR ECONOMIC DEVELOPMENT

IE NATURE OF THE PROBLEM

Economic issues are always central to politics, to be sure, but in
esent-day Latin America economic problems have taken on an
pecial urgency. The rate of population growth has accelerated, due
large part to the decrease in the death rate consequent on the
loption of preventive public health techniques, without any com-
nsating reduction in the birth rate. In other words, it is not enough
day for national production to grow; if it does not grow faster
an population, then despite increased production, per capita levels
consumption deteriorate. There are ever more mouths to feed,
icks to clothe, heads to shelter.

Not only are the problems themselves more acute, but the con-
iousness of their existence as problems for which remedies exist
as been heightened by developments in communications and travel
at repeatedly bring the suffering into confrontation with the com-
ortable. At the same time the evolution of the Soviet Union to a
osition from which its missionary message of material betterment

may be heard with both force and plausibility acts as a catalyst i inducing readiness to bring about change—to some extent for th forces within the Latin American countries seeking amelioration c conditions; more strongly for those in the United States and in th local upper classes fearful primarily of the extension of Soviet ir fluence.

The conditions that lead to low levels of production and lo standards of living in Latin America might be summarized briefl as follows, bearing in mind always that here we are generalizin and therefore necessarily over-simplifying. In the agricultural secto especially in the growing of food crops for local consumption, mo ern technique is generally not followed, production is not rationall organized, and incentives are lacking. The crops concentrated on fc export are however also those being increasingly produced, often a lower cost, by the countries of Africa and Asia; this means th steady long-term depression of prices. At the same time, given th fairly inelastic demand curves that exist for these products,[1] shor term fluctuations in supply result in drastic shifts in world marke prices, with a resultant inability to budget income over a longe period that renders rational planning extremely difficult.

Government policy, for its part, often does little to help. Taxatio is often counterproductive (in the form of export taxes, as in th case of Paraguay, for example, which may be easy to collect, an dependable as a source of revenue, but limit sales of the country products by raising the prices at which they are sold abroad). Ta policy is rarely set with a view to mobilizing capital and directing where it will most aid development.

THE IMPERATIVES OF ECONOMIC DEVELOPMENT POLICY

One of the striking features of the current phase of Latin Amer can history is that in embarking on programs of economic develo

[1] That is, demand does not change much in response to changes in pric the price of coffee has to drop a great deal before Brazil can sell addition amounts abroad. I have been prevailed on not to discuss possible remedi action through international agreement—commodity agreements, free tra areas, etc.—which would take the discussion too far afield.

ent, governments of all sorts find that, regardless of their ideologi-l orientations and policy preferences, the requirements of develop-ent impose certain imperatives of their own on the direction of licy.

This dynamic of the situation has had curious and spectacular sults. The same Arturo Frondizi who helped undermine Perón's sition with a powerful radio speech against the dictator's change policy toward permitting the exploitation of Argentine oil re-urces by foreign companies, for example, can find himself, four ars later, as President, inviting foreign oil interests to Argentina der favorable terms. Two years after commencing his term of fice by decreeing a 60 per cent general increase in wages, he can d himself using the army to break strikes called to back up union age demands.

Similarly, Juan Lechín Oquendo, the secretary-general of the olivian mineworkers' union and the country's Vice-President, rmerly a Trotskyite and an "anti-Yankee" economic nationalist, n find himself on a pilgrimage to Washington early in 1961 to try arrange for North American investment in Bolivia's ailing tin-ining industry. Clearly, one cannot argue with economics; one can ly obey—or rather, one can disobey only at the price of unpleasant nsequences. What, then, are these powerful and paradox-inducing nperatives that are imposed by a policy of economic development?

The *sine qua non* of economic development is investment. Devel-oment means the expansion of per capita production, year after ar; that is, a steady increase in productivity, the capacity to pro-ice. This increase has come about, in the developed countries, imarily through the increased use of machinery and the improve-ent of technique. This in turn means that current resources must devoted, as much as possible, not to consumption—the purchase manufacture of goods for immediate use—but to producer's goods tools, machinery, commercial buildings, transportation capacity—hich serve to increase future production.

One can raise investment funds either at home or abroad. We rn first to the problems of attracting foreign investment.

Foreign Investment. A policy of attracting investment fro abroad is faced with several political difficulties. In Latin Americ especially, there is an emotional resentment of foreign investme as such, partly for historical reasons, partly based on economic mi understanding, and partly based on genuine current grievances.

There is, first of all, the allegation that foreign investors interfe in the politics of the host country. Warrant for this charge ca certainly be found in the history of the foreign relations of the Lati American states. In the early years of the twentieth century, foreig holders of the bonds issued by the various governments of the are were uniformly successful in inducing their own governments t intervene on their behalf, by diplomatic representations and on occa sion by military action, when payment obligations on the bonc were not met. The "Roosevelt Corollary" to the Monroe Doctrin was occasioned by U. S. acknowledgement of the justice of th claims of the foreign bondholders, on the one hand, together wit reluctance to see European powers intervene in the Western Hem sphere, on the other. The administrations of Theodore Rooseve and Taft themselves took action to safeguard bondholders' interes by seizing customs houses (customs duties being at the time th chief source of public revenue) in Haiti, the Dominican Republi and Nicaragua; these customs receiverships developed into full-sca military occupations, the last of which was not finally liquidate until 1934.

Direct government action carried to the point of overt militar intervention on behalf of investors in the economy of another sta is today, clearly, a thing of the past. The fact that United State investors cannot count on automatic government intervention o their behalf was demonstrated by the Roosevelt administration policy of restraint toward the Mexican expropriation of foreign o interests in 1938. Nevertheless, the defense of investors' interest along with the protection of its citizens in their other activiti abroad, remains a routine concern of any foreign office; damage t those interests invariably occasions protest, and may result in general deterioration of relations between the states concerned.

Of course, foreign companies have been known to interfere in cal politics on their own without calling in the help of the home overnment. This type of practice occurred in most flagrant form uring the early years of the present century, and the latter part of ie nineteenth, perhaps with Samuel Zemurray (at the time, of tandard Fruit) the most notorious offender. Foreign companies no nger begin civil wars and equip one of the contending armies, as emurray is reputed to have done, but it would be unrealistic to ippose that they do not try to foster and protect their interests by olitical activities, just as domestic companies do.

One should not go to the other extreme, however, and think that reign economic interests, today, "give orders" to local governients. Competent and responsible governments can dictate to forgn companies the terms on which they will operate locally, with ie companies' only recourse to close down operations if the terms re too harsh; the government in power in 1958 in Venezuela evised in its own favor the arrangements under which foreign oil ompanies operated, for example, while Costa Rica, Panama, and Ionduras have taken similar action with relation to the banana ompanies. A corrupt and irresponsible political leadership may still e bribed by a foreign operator to accept unfavorable terms; but urely in such a case the fault lies only partly with the company.

Even during the period when the ownership of government bonds f the Latin American states by individuals and financial institutions 'as a major category of foreign investment in the area, direct ecoomic activity by foreign companies took place, principally in iining and the development of railroads. Direct investment today concentrated in two types of activity: the development of primary roduction—of crops and minerals, that is—for the export market; nd, more recently, in the manufacture of consumer goods and the rovision of services for the local market. Each of these types of ctivities has generated its own characteristic set of resentments on ie part of the Latin American populations.

In relation to the exploitation of mineral resources for export—il, metals, nitrates—the rather curious idea has evolved, somewhat similar to the attitude of a misguided wing of the North America conservation movement, that the "taking out" of the country of it natural resources for use elsewhere represents a kind of theft of th national patrimony. This attitude can be encountered in Argentin toward the foreign development of domestic oil deposits, for ex ample, but it is general, at a popular level, throughout the area. I economic terms this belief makes no sense, of course: a resourc lying untouched under the ground is without value—especially sinc technological developments may in any case render its use obsolet at some future date. The nation clearly benefits, in wages, ta revenues, government participation in the enterprise's profits, and raising of the general level of economic activity, by the exploitatio of the resource.

A further component of the generally unfavorable attitude t foreign investment common in the area is the feeling, comparab to one of the premises of Marxist economics, that any return o capital represents unjust exploitation; that only labor creates valu and therefore the interest and profits accruing to the provider c capital represents an unearned charge on the economy. From th viewpoint of capitalist economics, of course, this attitude misses th point: capital is a scarce resource and so must be attracted by a rat of compensation adequate to meet those offered by the competin demands for capital.

In addition, there are frequently present various specific grievance against individual foreign companies. One, the factual basis fc which is disappearing among the more enlightened foreign con panies, lies in the differential treatment of local and foreign en ployees in salaries, fringe benefits, and advancement to responsibl positions. Another, applying specifically to utilities companies, i directed against the rates charged, rate increases being clearly visibl and of widespread impact, and also against the quality of the servic provided; complaints on the latter score are quite likely to be wel founded, by the way.

One charge sometimes made against a foreign company engage in the production of the single crop on the export of which th country's economy largely depends is that its activities maintain the monocultural system with all the evils that attend it. It is difficult to see any justice in this charge, however, which amounts in effect to blaming the company for what other companies and individuals are *not* doing; except in the case that its activities actually prevent the economy from diversifying—if, for example, it monopolizes the country's land or other strategic resources. In such a case—as in others where a foreign company may justifiably bear blame—the local government is usually equally at fault for allowing a disadvantageous system to continue. Where competent, honest, and responsible governments exist, abuses of their position by foreign companies disappear quickly.

Such governments are unfortunately not the rule in Latin America as yet, and the suspicion of venal practice automatically attaches to government leaders whose relations with foreign business interests are close. Where a government tries to attract foreign investment by means of tax or other concessions, for example, a substantial segment of the population is ready to assume immediately that politicians have been bribed by foreign interests to make the concession in question.

Given the set of popular attitudes described, it is clear that substantial political pitfalls await governments that encourage foreign investment. The unpopularity of Perón's decision—after the deleterious effects of his economic policies had begun to make themselves felt—to invite North American companies to exploit Argentine oil deposits helped create the climate of opinion that contributed to his downfall. In this respect, as in others, Mexico's leadership has shown itself skilled and resourceful in developing a rational alternative to such self-defeating but popular gestures of economic nationalism, in the form of "Mexicanization." "Mexicanization"[2] means that no economic enterprise operating in Mexico may be controlled by foreigners; in other words, that decisions affecting the Mexican economy must be made only by Mexicans. This formulation clearly appeals to economic nationalism; but what the policy means in

[2] Not to be confused with nationalization.

practice is that at least 51 per cent of the stock of an enterprise must be owned by Mexicans. The only damage to the Mexican economy that might arise under this formula is that investments advantageous to the economy for which foreign capital was available might not be made because of a shortage of matching Mexican capital. In practice, this does not occur. The effect instead has been to channel Mexican capital into productive enterprise rather than non-productive by providing attractive investment opportunities in enterprises organized by reputable foreign firms manufacturing or marketing established products. It may also have been the case that the foreign capital available for investment in Mexico went twice as far as it would otherwise have done, whereas at the same time the sting was taken out of the irrational appeals of economic nationalism. The Chileans have refashioned their relations with the copper-mining companies along similar "partnership" lines, and other countries may follow.

It remains true, nevertheless, that the encouragement of foreign investment—chiefly, of course, North American—is a suspect or unpopular policy in Latin America.

Promoting Domestic Investment. One raises funds at home by forcing the reduction or postponement of consumption—this is the net effect of a government policy aimed at amassing capital for investment, regardless of the specific technique chosen. One can hold down wages, thus making funds available for business to invest itself; one can raise taxes, thus giving government an investable "surplus"; or one can create new currency by inflationary techniques (for example, printing new bills), which is similar in effect to a highly arbitrary tax—it makes money available to government by taking purchasing power from those groups and individuals that are least able to protect themselves against inflation.

The inflationary road represents the path of least resistance for governments desiring to raise funds. Its effects are not so immediately felt, and thus opposition not so easily aroused as by a wage freeze or a tax rise. As we shall see below, inflation has side effects that damage the prospects for development. Nevertheless, a certain amount of inflation is probably unavoidable in a developing economy. The problem is to try to hold it to a minimum.

Given the sheer magnitude of the task of developing the economies of Latin America, especially in view of the pressures of population rise, all potential sources of investment funds must be mobilized. Although this fact appears clear enough to an outsider, too many Latin Americans fall into the painless fallacy of assuming that the United States can inject enough dollars to do the job by itself. The Alliance for Progress program is clear on this point: the Latin American states cannot expect the United States to supply investment funds so long as domestic sources of genuinely surplus funds remain untapped.

It is not to be denied that there are indeed local funds in the countries of the area that are not being used to further development, even though they could be diverted to this use without causing any hardship whatsoever. The legendary anonymous Swiss bank accounts still play their part in absorbing the funds misappropriated by the betrayers of the public trust who are found all too frequently in the Latin American republics. Many Latin American investors put their money into securities of United States firms, presumably for safety's sake. Moreover, where those able to do so do invest in their own country's economy, the fields chosen are rarely the productive ones. For example, a typical contemporary use of investment funds is in the construction of luxury apartment buildings and hotels.

At the same time, some of the funds that might otherwise be used for investment are not invested at all but instead are expended on luxury items imported from abroad. This phenomenon constitutes not only a diminution of potential investment, but also a burden on the country's limited supply of foreign currencies, which would better be devoted to the import of goods that can aid the process of development.

Here clearly the nation will benefit from policies which seek to channel funds of this type into investment rather than consumption, and which conserve foreign exchange for the import of machinery and other items of strategic value for a development program. Tax and exchange control policies are appropriate tools for these purposes.

Monetary Stabilization. As was noted above, the danger of inflation is very great during the initial stages of a development program. Money is being spent on capital projects; that is, workers are receiving wages for constructing roads, buildings, and dams, none of which they can buy. The money they receive goes to buy the limited amount of consumers' goods available, and prices rise; an inflationary spiral begins. Accordingly, an anti-inflationary program, designed to maintain a stable value for the currency, is a necessary part of a policy for economic development. Without such a program, costs rise, and the development plan must be curtailed.

Furthermore, such investment as does take place during a period of continuing inflation will be misplaced, from the point of view of economic development, since it will be designed to be proof against future price rises. Here the luxury-apartment-house problem enters. If one invests in a factory, say, one can raise prices as inflation proceeds; but costs of labor and raw materials can be expected to rise, and minimize or wipe out profits. An apartment house, on the other hand, needs very little continuing expenditure —its chief cost is in the original construction. Thus the problem of rising costs is minimized, whereas rents can be steadily raised as inflation proceeds. An inflationary situation thus tends to channel investment, where that takes place, into non-productive uses.

A monetary stabilization program of this type needs to be introduced at other times too, of course, not only in conjunction with a development policy; during the last decade perhaps half of the Latin American countries have had to undertake rigorous stabilization programs, usually in cooperation with the International Monetary Fund, whose purpose it is to promote the continuing free convertibility of currencies.

What governmental actions are called for by the inauguration of a policy for monetary stabilization? Essentially, one must prevent rises in wages and prices, and reduce government expenditures to the level of income or below—that is, one must balance the budget. Although the elimination of inflation will lead to general benefits in the long run, a stabilization program indisputably imposes hardships and even suffering while it is first taking effect. Inflation is like a toothache, which hurts steadily, and is at the same time the symptom of an unhealthy condition which, if unattended, will lead to further physical deterioration. A stabilization program is like the extraction of an aching tooth, which may hurt excruciatingly while it is in progress, will require subsequent readjustment, but in the long run —if it is successful, and it may not be—is better both for health and for comfort.

Some typical features of recent stabilization programs in Latin America, which illustrate their unpopularity and thus the political dangers which they occasion, have been the following. A leading feature of the program embarked on by President Frondizi of Argentina was a freeze on wages, and he carried this to the point of calling out troops to break up violent demonstrations arising out of strikes staged in support of wage demands. The consequent difficulties he found in attempting a rapprochement with organized labor, and the support union members continued to vouchsafe to the neo-Peronists, were at the root of the action of the military in removing him from office in April of 1962.

The government of Jânio Quadros in Brazil attempted to pursue a policy of monetary stabilization that would repair the damage caused by the acute inflation that took place during the term of his predecessor, Juscelino Kubitschek. Among other features, the program involved the discharge of many government employees, and reductions in the pay of others, in the attempt to halt the printing of new currency that was the easy way out of its problems favored by the previous administration. President Quadros resigned his post, apparently in the unsuccessful attempt to get the Congress to vote him full legislative powers with which to implement his economic policies.

In Bolivia, the administration of President Siles Zuazo (1956-60) found itself under continual popular siege, as it were, in response to the President's attempt to halt the inflation that had sent the value of the boliviano from 1.5 to the dollar to 12,000 to the dollar in 20 years, and which had reached a runaway pace during the term of his predecessor. The Siles administration, in cooperation with the International Monetary Fund, not only tried to hold the line on wage increases for workers, including those in the government-owned tin mines, which clearly meant hardship for them and their families, but also removed most of the subsidies it had been making to hold down the prices of items for sale in the miners' commissaries. President Siles even resorted on two occasions to hunger strikes, in the courageous, and eventually successful, attempt to shame workers into giving up their wage demands, while demonstrating to the IMF the sincerity of his attempt to bring about monetary stabilization. This was a tragic situation for all concerned. There can be little doubt of the abject conditions of life of the miners, as indeed of most of the rest of the population of that unhappy country. From this point of view, their claims were certainly justified. Yet the state of the economy, and especially of the tin mines themselves, was such that it could not support any improvement in those conditions. If the stabilization program were successful, foreign financing could be obtained and used to advantage, it was hoped, in an attempt to rehabilitate the mines and begin the long climb to decent standards of life for the Bolivian people. This was a case of a very painful toothache, but also of an extremely painful extraction, with the prospect of a lengthy and problematical recovery.

POLITICAL PROBLEMS OF POLICY FOR ECONOMIC DEVELOPMENT

At the turn of the century a President named Porfirio Díaz was in office in Mexico, together with a group of technical aides who have gone down in history as the *científicos*. They earned the name by having as their intention to govern Mexico scientifically, that is, to allow their policies to be guided by the technical requirements of political and fiscal statecraft. The *científicos* were concerned that

Mexico's economy develop, and they embarked on programs adapted to this end, given what they believed to be the scientific knowledge of the time. Foreign investment was, of course, necessary, and was heavily favored by the laws. Drawing on the contemporary dogmas of what they took to be the scientific study of society, the government determined to enter upon no programs of social amelioration, which would destroy the autonomy of the marketplace (economics) and encourage idleness and immorality (sociology); although in any case no improvement could be wrought in the Indian, who was biologically inferior material (anthropology). Thus, the regime followed an authoritarian policy of repressing discontent while allowing very liberal concessions to foreign business interests—Mexico became "the mother of foreigners, the stepmother of Mexicans."

The danger of a new Porfirianism lurks in contemporary economic development policies, too. It is easy to interpret the technical requirements of a development program that includes monetary stabilization features as a purely "Right-wing" program designed in the class interest of the rich—easy, that is, for rich and poor alike. As was previously stated, such a program can be expected to entail such measures as a freeze on wages, a decrease in government spending on welfare programs, the reduction of the number of government employees and a lowering of the pay of the remainder, the maintenance or even imposition of taxes on the poor, together with the adoption of policies favorable to foreign and domestic investors. It is only natural that the well-to-do will embrace the program, protesting that they regret the necessity of receiving benefits for themselves while hardships are imposed on the poor, but that they make the sacrifice in the interest of developing the country; whereas the poor immediately see that what must have happened is that the government leaders have sold out to the bankers of Wall Street.

A development program in a free economy readily takes on a character of this kind; and not only in a free economy: the economic development of the Soviet Union, which proceeded almost entirely without foreign assistance, entailed greater sacrifices from the poor, especially from the peasants, than could have been imposed by a democratic government.

Two lines of policy are open to responsible democratic governments to soften these "Right-wing" effects of the development program. One is to lay stress on the "Left" measures that assist development; these exist, although to a lesser extent than those of Rightist implications. A measure of this kind already referred to is to limit the importation of luxury consumer's goods. Another is the expansion of educational facilities and programs, which can be regarded as a high-return investment in human beings. Another is land reform, which is taken up at greater length later.

The other line of policy is simply to conduct a program of social amelioration which does not in itself conduce to economic development—which will in fact, taken by itself, damage the development program, because it diverts resources that could otherwise have been used in investment. To embark on a social welfare program, in this context, means to slow development, other things being equal. Several observations need to be made on this point, however. One is that the purpose of the whole economic development policy is to raise standards for future generations; to adopt social welfare measures today slows the rate of progress but seems eminently just in that it ensures that the present generation will derive benefits from the process also. Clearly, one must not overdo expenditures on current programs, however, since it is possible to slow the rate of development to zero or to a negative figure, as was the case during the administration of Juan Perón.

Another argument may carry more force in this connection, however. Given the fact of political instability, it is quite feasible that the political disorder following on the consistent implementation of a purely "Rightist" development policy may cause the failure of the whole program—either by forcing a change of government or simply by itself consuming resources. For example: the government of Cheddi Jagan in British Guiana embarked on a development program at a maximum rate of speed, which called for sacrifices so unpopular that the costs of the destruction caused by the ensuing riots will set back the development program by two or three years. One is reminded of the man who proposed to save money by feeding his horse less; he saved a lot of money, but the horse died. One can develop an economy mightily only to have it collapse for "extraneous," but avoidable, reasons.

Taking this into consideration, it becomes clear that spending on housing, social services, etc., may actually be a rational charge on the economic development program, even in an accounting sense, if without it political disturbance would make the economic effort impossible or impose additional internal policing costs on the government.

LAND REFORM

Under the circumstances of land tenure most general in Latin America, a policy of land reform can provide the attractive prospect of at the same time promoting economic development, bringing about an immediate rise in living standards, fostering national integration, augmenting the government's popularity, reducing political violence, and contributing to human dignity. Whether these possibilities will all become actual depends, however, on the successful surmounting of a variety of obstacles.

Land reform means the transfer of the ownership of land to those who work it. Given the mode in which the overwhelming majority of the large estates of the southern part of the hemisphere are farmed, this can be expected to result in an increase of production; people work better when they are working for themselves, and not for others. If this occurs, production goes up, and the peasant eats better; he may have a surplus for sale, which goes to the city to feed workers in a new industry, perhaps; and so on. Now, several limitations of land reform need to be noted right away. One is that some crops, as we have seen, are rationally farmed on a large-scale basis; production drops if land in these crops is broken up into small parcels. Because of this, the Mexican land reform has retained intact some extremely large production units planted in cotton and hemp. The same comment applies to estates that are being rationally farmed with the aid of mechanized equipment. The latter constitute, however, a very small proportion of Latin American agricultural units.

For many reasons, it is easy for a land reform to fail completely. For example: the peasant needs to buy tools, seed, and fertilizer; he needs to feed his family; but he gets no income from his plot until the harvest. If the government does not provide credit at the same time as it distributes land, then the new landowner has to go into debt to the local moneylender, mortgaging his farm, say, until the harvest. Local rates of interest are exorbitant, becoming astronomical in some areas. If there is a crop failure, the peasant loses his land to the holder of the mortgage—and in the course of one or two generations the land becomes again concentrated in a few hands.

So provision must be made for credit facilities at the time of the land distribution. Agricultural extension services need to be provided, too, to acquaint the new smallholder with modern farm technique, if the government expects maximum agricultural production as an aid in the country's development program.

The Mexican, and now the Cuban, land reforms have partly eliminated the problem of reconcentration by limiting the scope of ownership of the distributed lands. In Mexico, the reform has (with ups and downs over the years) stressed the *ejido,* the system of village landholding in common. Under this system the land belongs to the village as a whole; the individual has a limited title to his plot, farming it and owning its produce but forbidden to dispose of the land. In Cuba the regime has established state farms alongside those individual holdings that are still permitted; in them the peasant is a worker employed by the state, and an owner only in the nominal sense that all citizens are owners of public concerns.

Problems also exist in connection with the compensation given to owners of the land. The Indian peasants who seize lands belonging to absentee landowners in the highlands of Peru don't perceive the existence of a problem here: the land has always been theirs but was simply taken from them by force at the time of the Conquest. This argument carries a certain amount of conviction. Nevertheless, the present owners do have a legal right to the land, which entitles them to compensation if the land is taken from them. Clearly, the government cannot pay cash on the land it expropriates; this would introduce a great deal of currency into the economy without a compensating increase in production, which means inflation. One can pay in bonds, instead of in cash—but if the bond does not mature for a long time (40 years, say), and meanwhile pays only 2 per cent interest, the landowner is getting very little indeed for his property. The issue of compensation thus becomes one of degree: how much should be paid, over what time span, and in what proportion payments should be made in cash. An arrangement very fair to the landowners—perhaps too fair, since it puts a strain on the national treasury—is that adopted in the Venezuelan land reform law of 1960, which in most cases provides for compensation one-third in cash, and two-thirds in long-term bonds.

The problem of fixing a price on the land to be expropriated can also create difficulties. The Guatemalan land reform of 1952, for example, took as its basis the assessed value of the holdings, which represented only a fraction of their market value.

Now that the Alliance for Progress program is in existence, and stipulates agrarian reform as one of the requirements a country must satisfy in order to receive U. S. aid, one has to beware of nominal agrarian reforms that on detailed inspection turn out to be no more than old-fashioned "boondoggles." Such a pseudo-reform might involve, say, the landowner's disposing of the barren sections of his property to the government (represented by his cousin, an official in the land reform agency) at an inflated price. In view of the fate of other well-conceived programs in Latin America, this kind of thing is far from being out of the question.

It is possible, nevertheless, for a responsible government to put through a land reform program that works, although the difficulties are substantial. If such a program is successful, it can not only raise the living standards of those directly involved, but also contribute to the economic growth of the country as a whole; it can give the peasants a new dignity and pride in themselves, while at the same time integrating their activities into the national economy and national life.

Whether a land reform program is feasible depends in part on the availability of arable land. Many of the countries of Latin America have unused land, at present inaccessible but usable if access roads are constructed. This is not the case in all of the republics, however. In Haiti, for example, where land ownership is already widely distributed, the problem is simply one of population density. There are just too many people for the available land, and as a result individual holdings are very small indeed.

The institution of the Alliance for Progress program, with its clearly announced intention of putting "strings" in the form of requirements for tax, land, and administrative reform, on United States aid to her southern neighbors, has placed new emphasis on one aspect of the policy-making process in the typical Latin American state. This is its responsiveness to foreign, as well as to domestic, constituencies. To be sure, it is true today that every small state —and every large one too, for that matter—must take into account the probable reactions from other countries to measures it contemplates taking. But the Latin American states, dependent as most of them are on the world market for their products and on the need for foreign investment, are under special constraints on this score. Countries' performance in meeting the conditions specified for receiving Alliance for Progress aid is now monitored by an inter-American committee functioning under the Organization of American States. This has had some beneficial effect in reducing the resentment, formerly directed exclusively at the United States, which is engendered by the necessity of having to take foreign views into account.

C. IN CONCLUSION: POLICY FOR POLITICAL DEVELOPMENT

THE PROBLEM IN PERSPECTIVE

Earlier in the book the concept of "political development" was introduced, to mean the evolution of social and political practice through stages correlating increasingly with both democracy and stability. Such evolution can come about through the emergence of secular economic and demographic trends; unbidden, increments in political development may arrive on the crests of waves of immigration, or be found on the peaks of economic booms. At the same time, it should be possible for political leaders to pursue policies deliberately designed to promote political development, just as today they feel they must adopt programs that will encourage economic development.

This has in fact occurred. As one looks at the countries that stand toward the "more advanced" end of the spectrum of political development in this light, it becomes clear that in several cases their favorable situation is due not only to advantageous economic and demographic factors, although these exist, but often to the deliberate action of some creative statesman who diagnosed his country's ills and brought about structural changes designed to remedy them. In Mexico, for example, Plutarco Elías Calles knew perfectly well what he was doing when he created the National Revolutionary Party in the wake of Obregón's assassination. In the radio speech Calles made explaining his move, he made clear that the formation of the party was an attempt to assure the peaceful succession to power while at the same time maintaining the social and economic goals of the Revolution, by making the transition from the era of personalism to the era of institutionalism.[3]

José Batlle y Ordóñez played a similar role in the history of Uruguay, although the manner of his approach was quite different. Batlle's place in Uruguayan history is due to his three great achievements: he ended the civil warfare between Colorados and Blancos that had been endemic until his Presidency; he was the architect of Uruguayan democratic socialism and the welfare state; and he introduced the idea of the collegial executive as a device to avoid the danger of dictatorship inherent in the institution of the strong Presi-

[3] Most observers have been rather skeptical of Calles' motivation here, interpreting his action in the light of his later behavior as "strong man." For reasons too complex to go into here, I am inclined to accept Calles' stated motives at face value.

dency. Under Batlle's guidance, Uruguay, too, took a giant step along the road to the goal of a stability that was combined with democracy and at the same time with social reform.

Alberto Lleras Camargo has attempted the same feat in Colombia, using still other methods. Hoping to put an end to party warfare and stabilize the succession to power by the National Front agreement, which provides for parity of the Conservatives and Liberals on all political bodies and the alternation of the Presidency between the parties, Lleras's success in the long run will depend on how well the National Front can satisfy popular demands for social and economic amelioration.

Judging by the features common to the examples given above, one could say that successful policies for political development of the past have (1) reduced the scope and intensity of conflict among parties and organized groups; (2) stabilized the succession to high office, while limiting the possibilities of the abuse of powers; and (3) promoted programs of social and economic welfare.

COMPLEMENTARY PERSPECTIVES ON THE PROBLEM

Subsidiary conclusions arrived at in other sections of the book converge on this definition of the basic problem of promoting political development as involving the attainment of an inter-group *modus vivendi,* the stabilization of democratic political institutions, and the adoption of a liberal social and economic policy as a permanent national goal; these are the three dimensions in which a high level of political development is attained. These three aspects are not separable from each other, but act in mutual support and reinforcement.

A thesis of this kind was implicit in the discussion of techniques for curbing the military influence in politics. It was remarked then that the best defense against the military ultimatum was in the last analysis popular support in the sense of willingness on the part of the general public to fight on behalf of the regime, whether or not actual fighting proved to be necessary. But the availability of such popular support depends after all on the government's pursuance of a generally accepted social policy that acknowledges the legitimate claims on government of the major population sectors, and especially—as we noted in the case of Mexico—of those able to use violence effectively. From the point of view of the groups to which the weapon of violence is available, they can forgo its use only on the assurance of a continuing respected voice in the processes of decision-making, an institutionalized place in an authentically constitutional state. The preservation of civilian supremacy, then, rests in a general sense on the regime's social policy, and on its representative character.

Similarly, from the individual's point of view, it is clear that loyalty to a system of government depends on the ability of that system to satisfy needs felt to be legitimate. Loyalty to constitutional forms in themselves certainly exists, but with the marked tendency of being considered secondary to the protection of one's concrete interests.[4] Put briefly: one defends an order of things in which one has a stake. Herein lies the connection between political stability and social reform, which becomes clearer if one considers the political effects of land reform. Farmers, as experience everywhere shows, can be either very radical or very conservative. One way to shift peasants from one end of the political spectrum to another, to make conservatives out of revolutionaries, is by giving them the land they work, converting proletarians into propertyholders.[5]

From yet another perspective: that general acknowledgement of the legitimacy of a regime that is the best long-run assurance of stability can come today, given present-day attitudes, only when institutions are founded on principles of democracy and social welfare; in other words, where all population elements have a voice in policy, and government fosters the well-being of all.

A policy for political development, to summarize, involves the pacification of the major population groups by conferring on each

[4] This is clearly visible in the United States in attitudes toward the Supreme Court. The conservative who defended the Court's constitutional role when it was nullifying New Deal legislation attacks it when it outlaws segregation.

[5] A good illustration of this is the change in the political attitudes of the peasantry during the French Revolution.

of them a role in the institutionalized processes of decision-making and a stake in a socioeconomic order constructed along equitable lines. There is no incompatibility, at this level, between the goals of democracy, stability, and welfare; to the statesman's eye they blend into a single historic aim.

It is possible to meet these historic needs spuriously, to make a show of their attainment that is really a false one, capable, in the long run, only of retarding genuine political evolution. This possibility, in our time, has been raised by the Peronistas on the Right and the Fidelistas on the Left. But their claims to satisfy the needs of the time are based on force and fraud. The regime of each purchases what stability it has only with the use of force, however discriminatingly or intermittently it is used; the claim of each to be "truly" democratic, without fair elections and civil liberties, clearly rests on fraud—on misrepresentation and double-talk; their ability to satisfy the people's economic requirements rests on fraud in the one case and force in the other—Perón created a transient lower-class prosperity that was based on consuming capital and thus could not last; Fidel Castro may eventually succeed, if he remains in power, in raising the living standards of the Cuban peasants, but he will be able to maintain himself through the interim period of dislocation attendant on the conversion to an operating socialist economy only through the extensive use of coercion, which has become a need that feeds on itself.

The existence of the spurious and the genuine answers to the needs of the historic moment provides at the same time the danger and the hope—taken together, the challenge—of Latin American politics in our time.

Suggested for Further Reading

Bemis, Samuel Flagg, *The Latin American Policy of the United States,* Harcourt Brace, New York, 1943. Detailed history, favorable to the United States.

Crawford, William Rex, *A Century of Latin American Thought,* Harvard, Cambridge, 1944. First-rate intellectual history.

Davis, Harold E., ed., *Government and Politics in Latin America,* Ronald, New York, 1958. Treatment by topics.

Hanke, Lewis, *America: Continent in Ferment,* 2 vols., Van Nostrand, Princeton, 1960. Succinct surveys by country.

Hanson, Simon G., *Economic Development in Latin America,* Inter-American Affairs Press, Washington, 1951.

Heath, Dwight B., and Adams, Richard N., ed., *Contemporary Cultures and Societies of Latin America,* Random House, New York, 1965. Well-chosen collection of articles, mostly by anthropologists.

Johnson, John J., ed., *Continuity and Change in Latin America,* Stanford, Stanford University Press, 1964. A symposium dealing with the key actors—the student, the military, etc.

Johnson, John J., *Political Change in Latin America,* Stanford, 1958. An interesting interpretation of developments since 1900 in several key countries.

Lieuwen, Edwin, *Arms and Politics in Latin America,* rev. ed., Praeger, New York, 1961.

Mecham, J. Lloyd, *Church and State in Latin America,* University of North Carolina Press, Chapel Hill, 1934.

Needler, Martin C., ed., *Political Systems of Latin America,* Van Nostrand, Princeton, 1964. Country-by-country survey.

Pierson, William W., and Gil, Federico G., *Governments of Latin America,* McGraw-Hill, New York, 1957. Solid treatment by topics.

Schurz, William Lytle, *Latin America: A Descriptive Survey,* Dutton, New York, 1949.

Tomasek, Robert B., ed., *Latin American Politics,* Doubleday Anchor. Garden City, 1966. A collection of worthwhile readings.

Index

NOTE:

Hispanic surnames are sometimes "composite," that is, both father's and mother's family names are used. Thus the family name of Adolfo López Michelsen is *López;* his father's name was Alfonso López Pumarejo. Accordingly, both would be found listed under *L.* In addition, some family names are themselves "composite," and a double surname is handed down through the male line, for example, Miró Quesada, a famous family name in Peru. The situation is further complicated because many political figures do not normally use the mother's name; others use more than one *Christian* name; still others, especially in Brazil but also elsewhere, are known commonly by their Christian names only. The hapless speaker of English just has to get used to this as best he can. The author's favorite example of the diversity with which one can be confronted is a poster he saw in Lima urging the voters to support the APRA ticket in the 1962 elections. The names of the party's candidates for President and First and Second Vice-Presidents were listed thus:

VICTOR RAUL
MANUEL SEOANE
ARCA PARRO

The top line gives the Christian names of the party's Presidential candidate, Haya de la Torre; the middle line gives the Christian name and the family name of the candidate for First Vice-President; the bottom line gives the composite surname of the third man on the party ticket.